MAR 0 9 2005

Portfolios Matter

Portfolios Matter

What, Where, When, Why and How to Use Them

SHIRLEY-DALE EASLEY

KAY MITCHELL

Pembroke Publishers Limited

To my grandson, Jordan, who is just beginning his journey
as a life long learner.

To my husband, my best friend, Bob Mitchell for his patience and support.

To my daughter, Suzanne and son-in-law, Dan for always being there.

Kay

To my children, Rob, Tom and Julie, for standing beside me through thick
and thin and for teaching me that all things are possible.

To my mother, Eleanor Belmore, for instilling a love of
learning in all of her children.

Shirley-Dale

© **2003 Pembroke Publishers**
538 Hood Road
Markham, Ontario, Canada L3R 3K9
www.pembrokepublishers.com

Distributed in the U.S. by Stenhouse Publishers
477 Congress Street
Portland, ME 04101
www.stenhouse.com

We acknowledge the financial support of the Government of Canada through the Book Publishing Industry Development Program (BPIDP) for our publishing activities.

We acknowledge the Government of Ontario through the Ontario Media Development Corporation's Ontario Book Initiative.

National Library of Canada Cataloguing in Publication

Easley, Shirley-Dale
    Portfolios matter : what, where, when, why and how to use them /
Shirley-Dale Easley, Kay Mitchell.

Includes bibliographical references and index.
ISBN 1-55138-151-6
    1. Portfolios in education. 2. Students—Rating of. I. Mitchell, Kay
II. Title.

LB1029.P67E27 2003   371.26   C2002-906054-0

Editor: Cynthia Young
Cover Design: John Zehethofer
Cover Photography: Ajay Photographics
Typesetting: Jay Tee Graphics Ltd.

Printed and bound in Canada
9 8 7 6 5 4 3 2 1

Acknowledgments

We are indebted to the hundreds of teachers who have attended our workshops for sharing their ideas and asking insightful questions. It is the questions they asked that inspired us to take an in-depth look at our answers. The exploration and research that followed led to the writing of this book.

We would like to thank the teachers in our school for their support in our search for a better way to improve assessment. We were all learners as well as teachers and the collegiality that existed throughout the years encouraged us to persevere. We are especially grateful for the unwavering support and enthusiasm from our colleagues, Brenda Ward and Sandra McNeill.

We thank the children in our classrooms, wherever they are now, for their boundless energy, their trust and their willingness to try new ideas with eagerness and imagination.

We appreciate the support and feedback we received from the parents of our students. They provided constructive criticism and encouragement for our project from its infant stages to its full development.

We acknowledge the help we received from the following individuals at the Department of Education in New Brunswick, Canada: Tom Hanley, Director of Professional Development and Innovations, for his continued support and interest in all of our ideas and professional endeavors, Darlene Whitehouse-Sheehan, Assistant Director of Educational Programs and Services, for encouraging us to share our experiences and knowledge with other educators by providing the opportunity for our very first workshops, Colleen Sprague, Assistant Director of Evaluation, for guiding us through the process of assessment on a provincial level.

We thank Sheree Fitch, who planted the idea of writing a book and steered us in the direction of Pembroke Publishers.

We would like to express our thanks to Mary Macchiusi for her insight, encouragement and guidance and to Cynthia Young for her careful reading and editing of the manuscript.

And our warmest gratitude goes to Julie Easley and Bob Mitchell, our listeners, our critics, our runners, our drivers and our confidants. Their tireless commitment to helping us get this project completed is well above and beyond the call of duty.

Contents

Introduction

November 6. I am still working on report cards. The school is silent. Most of the teachers have gone home by now. The rain is beating against the windows and it is almost dark. Papers, last year's report cards, work files and folders surround me. There is an eerie feeling here in the school, and I am uneasy, not only about the weather, but also about the marks I am giving to my grade 2 students. I have to get back to work and stop pondering this. Why is it taking me so long this year? Why am I questioning everything? Do the piles of tests I am reviewing truly represent what the children know and can do? Am I being fair?

Kay

November 6. I stayed at school to finish my grade 6 report cards and I cannot seem to get them finished. It is cold and the wind outside isn't helping. I think I am looking at too many of last year's report cards for these students and it's bothering me. Why aren't my marks closer to the marks they got last year? Why are there so many discrepancies? I just walked down the hall and was surprised to see that Kay was battling with the same evaluation code. What is an 80 percent? What does this C+ mean? What is a 60 percent? Does my E for excellent mean the same as an E given by another teacher? I said, "I wish I could see their last year's work. What we need is evidence, we need proof." Kay laughed and said, "The proof is in the pudding."

Shirley-Dale

Little did we know that this one line, this one discussion, would lead us into several years of concentrated study on portfolio assessment and student-led conferencing. It was the beginning of all the research and work that eventually led us to seven years of conducting staff development workshops for educators. The workshops, entitled, *The Proof Is In The Pudding: Portfolio Assessment and Student-Led Conferences,* opened the door to the development of a number of other workshops associated with that topic.

The first step was to convince our colleagues that our current assessment practices were not keeping pace with the changes occurring in teaching and learning. In this infant stage of our exploration, we thought convincing the other teachers would be a simple task. We thought it was just a matter of having teachers learn new methods of assessment. At the time, we had no idea that to change the way we were assessing meant to change our basic assumptions about teaching and learning. It was our basic philosophy that had to change.

We facilitated five workshops in our school, using a co-research model. In a co-research model, all staff members have equal status in that each has the opportunity to contribute. We discovered that teachers, just as students in our classrooms, are at different levels of learning and readiness to accept new initiatives. However, by supporting each other in our early attempts, gathering pertinent literature for continued study and inviting experts as guest speakers at our round-table discussions, we had enough confidence to begin the process in our classrooms. Gradually, over a period of seven years, we evolved to whole-school implementation of portfolio assessment and, eventually, to student-led conferences.

As interest grew in our district and our province, the two of us were asked to plan and deliver portfolio assessment workshops to a wide range of people. To date, we have delivered the in-service sessions to more than 1500 teachers, administrators, parents, university students and international educators. Again, we discovered that all educators are at various stages of learning and levels of understanding. In our sessions, it is very important for us to meet participants at their own levels. In order to do this we give them opportunities to brainstorm and write down their questions. Their questions then become the focus of the presentation. It is interesting to note that, in the hundreds of questions that we have collected and analyzed throughout the years, they continue to evolve from and revolve around the same issues time after time. We have identified these issues and arranged the questions asked most often so that the "how-to" information facilitates teachers' understanding and implementation of portfolio assessment.

In this book, *Portfolios Matter: What, Where, When, Why, and How to Use Them*, we explore the answers to those questions one by one. We offer research-based, classroom tested and practical answers based on our many years of studying the subject, working in classrooms as teachers and presenting professional development to hundreds of educators. Throughout this whole process, we documented our own growth and development with personal journals.

This book outlines the steps for implementing a portfolio program as an integral part of the curriculum. We discuss the importance of developing and using criteria charts in a classroom, and provide samples of students' work showing growth and progression over time. In addition, we look at various methods of conferencing with parents. This book can be used as a guide for promoting staff development with a whole-school approach. We also offer excerpts from our journals over the years so the reader may accompany us on our journey, maneuvering around the roadblocks and sharing the successes along the way. In these writings, we strongly emphasize the need not only to understand and believe the philosophy behind this approach, but to persevere over time. This will be the most important key to success.

1

Balanced Learning and Portfolios

The grade, like the final score
of a game, never taught anyone
how to win or why they lost.
> – Lucas, 1992

November 30. It is amazing to me how much power that a report card still holds. In the days when I was in school, report card day was a monumental occasion, and it still is. I can remember the feeling that it stirred up inside of me, even the thought of taking it home. Butterflies in my stomach, I clutched the unopened envelope, with no idea what was in it or what my parents' reactions would be. Their expectations were extremely high. I knew that I had passed the tests, but it was still the teacher's secret that was hidden inside. From the discussions that I have just had with the parents in my own classroom, I realize that the aura surrounding the report card is as strong as ever.

Kay

November 30. It is only the first reporting period of the year, and I can't believe how many parents have asked if their child is going to pass or fail. Regardless of anything else that is happening in the classroom, it always comes back to that one question, "Will my child pass or fail?" I know it's a valid question, but, to me, it's almost like asking "Guilty or not guilty?" in a courtroom. I am both the judge and the jury. I wield all the power and I'm a little uneasy about it. Have I investigated thoroughly? Is the evidence substantial? What can I do to alleviate some of my control over a process that is so important?

Shirley-Dale

Finding a Balance in Today's Classrooms

Finding a balance connotes finding equilibrium or a sense of completeness. In all facets of life, people search for "balance." People try to eat a balanced diet as part of a healthy lifestyle. Many attempt to balance work with family responsibilities and their social lives. On a day-to-day basis, teachers strive to create and maintain balance in all the attributes of an effective and rich learning environment.

In the past, the teacher was not expected to perform such a "balancing act." Teaching practice was grounded in an educational philosophy that assumed there was a certain body of knowledge and skills that students must acquire. The teacher's task was to impart that knowledge to the students, who were passive learners. They were expected to master that body of content and they either passed or failed according to required standards before moving to the next grade.

In recent years, our understanding of the learning process has changed. Greater emphasis is placed on teaching and learning strategies that provide students with first-hand exploration and observation, conceptual understanding, problem solving, the use of a wide range of resource materials and collaborative group work. The focus is on teaching and learning for "real world" or authentic purposes with value placed on understanding, risk-taking, responding and discovering. The teacher is responsible for creating an interactive learning program by balancing many components in order to obtain a complete and comprehensive profile of each student's progress.

How do assessment and evaluation fit into a balanced learning program?

Teachers are continually assessing student performance, either formally or informally, throughout the school year. This is called formative assessment. At reporting time the information that has been gathered from various sources is used to make a professional judgment in the form of a final grade or a final mark. This process is called summative assessment or evaluation.

Traditionally, teachers were the only ones in the classroom with the authority to evaluate. Tests were administered at the end of a unit and at the end of the year, and, with the exception of marks on various projects, this was the only data the teacher collected to form the final mark. Such tests provided a limited picture of the students' full ability and performance level, and the information they provided came too late to be of use in curriculum or instructional planning. Yet, the process was uncomplicated and easy for parents to understand.

Traditional assessment procedures alone are not adequate to measure students' progress in a balanced learning program. For an environment that offers more authentic learning opportunities, educators have been required to develop a broad range of assessment strategies and techniques to augment traditional testing procedures.

Traditional vs. Authentic Assessment

Traditional Assessment	Authentic Assessment
Tests a certain body of knowledge	Set up tasks that replicate real-life challenges
Passive process	Active process
Recall/select questions	Critical/evaluative thinking, inquiry
Defined amount of time	Progressive
Individual attempt	Individual and collaborative attempts
Teacher controlled	Shared between student and teacher
Marking/grading over-emphasized	Curriculum tasks assessed
No self-evaluation	Student-evaluation valued

Using *only* traditional assessment approaches or *only* authentic assessment approaches provides only a partial picture of the student's proficiency. To believe that there is no specific body of knowledge to be learned, for example, is as counter-productive as believing that there are only facts to be assessed. A program that uses only one method or procedure is not a balanced assessment program. Teachers can develop a more balanced assessment program if they amalgamate procedures and methods that are consistent with the best available research on assessment. Their student assessments will be more successful and accurate.

Evaluation has become a more complex procedure in recent years. Firstly, teachers are required to make major decisions as to which methods of assessment best measure particular outcomes, and what weight the score from each method will have in the final mark. Secondly, teachers must use the information to evaluate the success of their own teaching, modifying procedures and curriculum when necessary. Finally, they must communicate and justify, to parents, the underlying principles of their assessment process, supplying concrete evidence of the student's progress and achievements.

From the Files

The Challenge Presented by Report Card Marks

Does a report card mark represent what a student really knows and can do?

A mark on a report card gives little in the way of concrete evidence regarding the students' accomplishments and where improvement is needed. It is just a mark. Although parents are more comfortable with marks and believe they know what marks convey from one year to the next, there could be huge variations in how they were compiled.

Why can a student's report card marks be so different from one year to the next?

This question has plagued educators and parents for many years. There are a number of possible explanations.

- Different teachers may have different values, and thus they might weigh the information collected differently.
- Teachers might be making subjective judgments, unintentionally rating students on factors that are not in a rubric.
- There may be a huge disparity in the knowledge base about curriculum outcomes and pedagogy among teachers on one staff, from school to school and from district to district.
- Teachers may be relying on dissimilar sets of criteria for their assessment and evaluation procedures, which leads to irregularities in marks.
- Students may be unaware of the specific criteria the teacher is using to judge their work.

Inconsistencies between the expectations of different teachers can lead to very different evaluations of the same student from one grade to the next. There is a definite need for teachers to agree on common principles, to establish and clearly define learning/achievement criteria and to ensure that evaluation procedures remain constant.

ACHIEVEMENT refers to pupil's performance at level of instruction. | EFFORT: refers to a pupil's effort in comparison with apparent ability

Evaluation Code

ACHIEVEMENT	EFFORT & INTEREST
E – Excellent	O – Outstanding
VG – Very Good	VG – Very Good
G – Good	G – Good
M – Minimum/Fair	NI – Needs Improvement
N/S – Not Satisfactory	

LANGUAGE ARTS

Program: Regular ☒   Effort [VG]

Other ☐

Listening Skills

Attends to Oral Presentations [G]

Follows Oral Directions [VG]

Speaking Skills

Vocabulary Development [VG]

Expression of Ideas [E]

Insightful!

Reading Skills

Word Attack Skills [VG]

Comprehension [E]

Oral Reading [E]

Uses a variety of strategies to decode.

Writing Skills

Printing/Writing [G]

Written Expression [E]

Printing is neat. Takes his time.

Spelling

Assigned Spelling

Application [G]

MATHEMATICS

Concepts [E]   Effort [VG]

Facts [E]

Problem Solving [E]

Math activities are above + beyond Grade two level.

The following are expressed in terms of Effort and Interest only

SUBJECTS		WORK AND SOCIAL HABITS	
Science	[VG]	Attentiveness	[G]
Health	[VG]	Works Independently	[G]
Social Studies	[VG]	Works Carefully	[G]
Art	[VG]	Class Assignments	[VG]
Music	[VG]	Home Assignments	[VG]
Physical Ed.	[VG]	Courteousness	[VG]
French	[／]	Conduct	[VG]
		Accepts Responsibility	[VG]

COMMENTS

Jack has successfully met all Grade two requirements with ease. In many Language Arts and Math activities, he has surpassed expectations. He's a joy to teach.

This is year-end report card for Jack, a grade 2 student. Jack's teacher selected the accompanying writing sample as representative of Jack's developmental level.

June 17

I akst my dad if i could feed the fira. He sid yes. But i was a little sard. But i gat over my fri

This piece of writing, according to Jack's teacher, not only met, but "surpassed," grade–level expectations.

ACHIEVEMENT refers to pupil's performance at level of instruction.		EFFORT: refers to a pupil's effort in comparison with apparent ability	

Evaluation Code

MATHEMATICS

ACHIEVEMENT	EFFORT & INTEREST
E – Excellent	O – Outstanding
VG – Very Good	VG – Very Good
G – Good	G – Good
M – Minimum/Fair	NI – Needs Improvement
N/S – Not Satisfactory	

Concepts	G	Effort	VG
Facts	M		
Problem Solving	M		

LANGUAGE ARTS

Program: Regular ☑ Effort ☐

Other ☐

The following are expressed in terms of Effort and Interest only

SUBJECTS HABITS		WORK AND SOCIAL	
Science	VG	Attentiveness	G
Health	G	Works Independently	NI
Social Studies	G	Works Carefully	NI
Art	G	Class Assignments	NI
Music	G	Home Assignments	VG
Physical Ed.	G	Courteousness	O
French	n/a	Conduct	O
		Accepts Responsibility	VG

Listening Skills

Attends to Oral Presentations	G
Follows Oral Directions	M

Speaking Skills

Vocabulary Development	G
Expression of Ideas	G

Reading Skills

Word Attack Skills	M
Comprehension	M
Oral Reading	M

Writing Skills

Printing/Writing	G
Written Expression	G

Spelling

Assigned Spelling	M
Application	M

COMMENTS

Anne has worked hard this year. She needs individual help with new concepts in Math and Language Arts. She should read during the summer for enjoyment to help increase her vocabulary and comprehension. I have enjoyed working with Anne.

The year-end report card for Anne, another grade 2 student, with a different teacher than Jack's.

ME AND MY NANNY

June 15

One day, me and my nanny went to the mall and we had fun we bought sum thing for my mom she bought a book box for her books. Then we went home and we made sum cookes for me and her they wer good and I hade one more for my mom I Love my nanny and my mom oh nanny mom is here she game she bought a book fror me I game and tood her that I made a cookes for her she liked it was raey good. mom said where are we going I sad. We are going home mom said oh no I forgot to get my book nanny got me and donot

The teacher chose this sample of writing to demonstrate Anne's writing competency at the end of the school year. Her teacher considered Anne's writing ability to be "good."

Why was Anne's writing only "good," while Jack's was deemed to be "excellent"? A comparison of the two pieces of writing shows clearly that Anne's writing ability is superior to Jack's. These two teachers had very different expectations for grade 2 students. The grade 3 teacher who will be teaching these students the following year could well, on the basis of this report card, make the judgment that Anne will need extra help in class. Jack, however, appears to be working at a higher level of achievement. Upon further inquiry, it was revealed that Anne's teacher was using set criteria to evaluate her writing. Jack's teacher was measuring his achievement by comparing it to other members of the class.

Discrepancies can sometimes arise when a student moves from one school district to a different one. In one case, a student named Jane moved from one school district to another in the summer between grades 4 and 5. Her report cards represented very different perceptions of the same student.

There were no samples of work included with Jane's grade 4 report card when she moved to her new school. Without any samples of Jane's grade 4 writing, it was natural for Jane's grade 5 teacher to expect, on the basis of Jane's grade 4 year-end marks, that Jane was a fairly competent student. However, Jane's first-term report card for grade 5 indicates a significant drop in both achievement and effort.

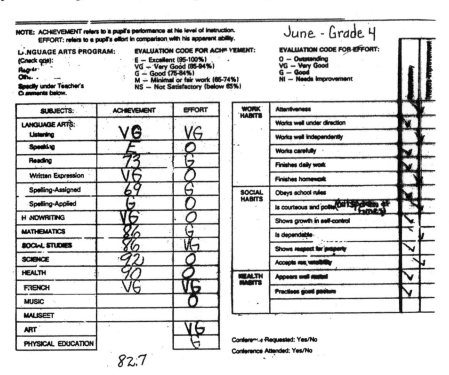

Jane's year-end report card for grade 4

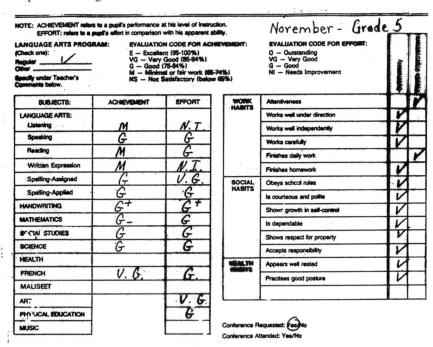

Jane's first-term report card for grade 5 at her new school

Jane's parents were confused and rightly so. They expressed displeasure and questioned the teaching ability, not of the grade 4 teacher, but of the grade 5 teacher. However, the grade 5 teacher had a writing sample to show the parents as evidence of Jane's level of writing competence. The criteria used to judge this sample of writing were shared with the parents, as well. It turned out that Jane's grade 4 teacher had judged her writing competency according to the improvement Jane had shown throughout the year. Jane's grade 5 teacher was part of a staff that had been involved in a series of in-service sessions on writing criteria and, through collaboration, had examined and critiqued numerous writing samples at various grade levels. Without samples of Jane's work from grade 4, the grade 5 teacher could only assess Jane's writing against the criteria the staff had developed. And those criteria were obviously different from the criteria Jane's grade 4 teacher had considered.

Sometimes students will rise or fall to the occasion, depending on the expectations of the teacher. These expectations are sometimes apparent in the kinds or levels of questions that the teacher asks. A case in point is Susan, a junior-level student who consistently received report card marks that were in the superior range throughout her school years. However, by comparing the two writing samples shown below, it is readily apparent that there is regression in the quality of Susan's writing. It appears that in grade 6, Susan was quite capable of critical thinking and of expressing her thoughts at a high level of competency.

The difference in quality and the kind of content in the two writing samples suggests that the grade 6 teacher was attuned to the developmental levels of learning and had set standards that challenged Susan to work at her optimum level. On the other hand, it seems that the grade 8 teacher had been asking mainly literal questions, requiring only short, simple answers. During her first grade 8 school term, Susan was working below her actual ability level. Susan's actual ability had not changed, but the quality and/or level of the questions or the standards of the teachers differed.

A writing sample from Susan's grade 6 reading log entry.

A writing sample from Susan's grade 8 reading log entry.

These kinds of inconsistencies in expectations are prevalent in many schools at all grade levels. The report card mark alone does not reveal the standards that the teacher is using to judge the student's level of achievement. Concrete evidence is needed to support the mark and to represent what the student knows and can do. One of the best methods for collecting and presenting that evidence is the process of making and maintaining a portfolio.

Balanced Assessment in a Balanced Learning Program

What is a balanced program of assessment?

A balanced program of assessment does not emphasize only one assessment approach or procedure. Instead, several methods of assessment are employed to give the most accurate overall picture of the student and his or her abilities. The final report card mark comes closer to representing and communicating what a student knows and can do if the teacher has gathered a wide array of information about the student. The quality of the information gathered is equal to the quality or fairness of the evaluation. It is somewhat like putting together a jigsaw puzzle. The more pieces that are put in place, the more clearly the whole picture can be seen. The greater the variety of assessment techniques, the greater the teacher's knowledge of the students and their abilities.

The Components of a Balanced Assessment Approach – A balanced assessment approach is an integral part of a balanced learning program. Assessment tools must be appropriate to the learning. Student achievement for different skills,

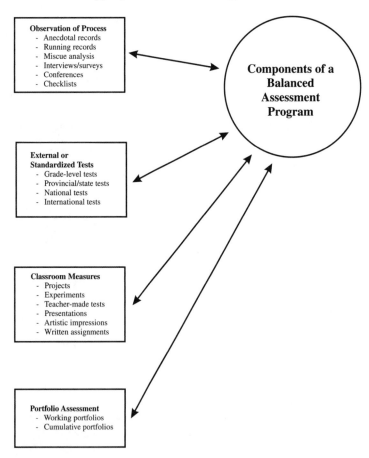

Observation of Process
- Anecdotal records
- Running records
- Miscue analysis
- Interviews/surveys
- Conferences
- Checklists

External or Standardized Tests
- Grade-level tests
- Provincial/state tests
- National tests
- International tests

Classroom Measures
- Projects
- Experiments
- Teacher-made tests
- Presentations
- Artistic impressions
- Written assignments

Portfolio Assessment
- Working portfolios
- Cumulative portfolios

Components of a Balanced Assessment Program

Equipment/Supplies

- Prepare and use checklists of specific things to be observed.
- Write in notebooks organized with a specific area for each student.
- Write on sticky notes and transcribe comments into a permanent file later.
- Wear a pen and notepad on a string.

The Approach

- Identify the purpose of the observations.
- Let students know what you are doing.
- Use highly descriptive language in notes.
- After several observations, review the notes, looking for patterns.
- Enter the student's name and put the date on all entries.

Time Considerations

- Schedule observation-times periodically during class sessions.
- Spend five minutes per student when making observations.
- Observe one or two students each day during normal activities.
- Observe one or two students during individual and group activities.

concepts and knowledge can be assessed and evaluated best with the right kind of assessment tools. For example, factual recall could be tested with short answer questions in an oral or written test. Drawings or manipulatives could be used in a hands-on environment to test math skills.

Observation of Process – One of the best ways to discover if a student can perform a task is to observe and write notes while the students are engaged in the specific activity. Observation of process can include anecdotal notes, checklists, interviews, conferences, listening to and analyzing the response of students and making notes on students' work or behavior on a daily basis. Using a systematic approach to note your observations of students will make this component more effective and efficient.

Classroom Measures – These measures include tests, projects, experiments, presentations, artistic impressions and written assignments. The tests can be prepared by the teacher, or may be supplied by a publisher to accompany a textbook. These components are important elements when examining student understanding of a concept, and, subsequently, for informing future instruction. When designing these assessment tools, teachers should bear in mind that the kinds of questions asked have a major influence on the effectiveness of the assessment process and outcomes.

The quality of the questioning is equal to the caliber of the results. Teachers who employ a combination of literal, inferential and critical/evaluative questions on classroom tests will gain a better understanding of the students' ability and knowledge than will teachers who ask only one level of questioning. If students are given opportunities to engage in all levels of questioning daily, and then are given adequate test-taking practice, classroom standards should surpass those expected on external tests.

Classification of Questions

Type of Question	Characteristics
Literal **Example:** What is the dog's name?	• "right there" questions • involve recalling, remembering, recognizing, defining, and identifying information • answer is stated explicitly in the text • words in the question match words in the text • often multiple choice, short answer or fill in the blank
Inferential **Example:** How do you know…?	• "think and search" questions • answer is in the text, but not stated explicitly • may need to read several paragraphs to relate various pieces of information • answer fills out what lies between the facts, sorts out and elaborates
Critical/Evaluative **Example:** How do you explain…? How is it connected to your life?	• "on my own" questions • answer is not explicitly stated in the text, but is inside the reader's head • challenge existing thinking and encourage reflection • may be more difficult to answer • require thinking skills

External Tests – This term refers to standardized tests. Often, standardized tests are administered at specific grade levels, on a worldwide, national, provincial or statewide basis. It is important for curriculum makers to get a snapshot of an entire region when evaluating the effectiveness of curriculum documents and the professional-development needs of the educators. Data generated from the results of external tests are analyzed to identify areas that need improvement in a broad perspective.

Even when the test results do not directly affect the report card marks of the students, the results are used to identify specific areas that need improvement, to revise curriculum to make changes in instruction and teaching methodologies, to examine teacher expectations and to raise standards in a particular school or region.

Portfolio Assessment – The student portfolio is the only assessment tool whereby the students and teachers act as partners in the assessment process. It is an authentic form of assessment, allowing students to learn skills that will be valuable throughout their lives. It is within this process that students learn to make decisions about their own learning, based on certain standards and to set goals for the future. A portfolio is a purposeful selection of a student's work that displays his or her efforts, progress and achievements. The items in the portfolio serve as evidence of the student's capabilities and developmental levels. The active involvement of students is crucial in portfolio assessment. The student chooses the items for the portfolio, reflects on and justifies the choice, and develops new learning goals based on his or her achievements.

What weight is given to each component of a balanced assessment program to get the final mark?

There is no precise formula for determining the weight of each component included to arrive at the final report card mark. All of the components are important and each plays a significant role in the reporting process. This is where the professional judgment of the teacher comes into play. Just as a doctor makes a professional judgment in diagnosing a specific ailment and deciding on treatment, a teacher matches specific learning outcomes with the appropriate assessment procedure.

What are the teacher's responsibilities in developing a balanced assessment program?

In order to develop a balanced assessment program, the teacher must:

- study curriculum documents.
- develop an understanding of various assessment techniques.
- choose the most appropriate forms of assessment to match the desired learning expectations.
- have a firm grasp of established standards that define proficiency in each curriculum area.
- study developmental levels of learning.
- encourage students to take risks and allow them time to practice before testing.
- use the most relevant, the most consistent and the most recent evidence to judge the developmental levels of learning for each student.
- award the final evaluation or mark accordingly.

January 20. I just finished reading my fifth article on Portfolio Assessment. I have come to believe it is an essential component in looking at the whole picture of a child's progress. Shirley-Dale and I have decided to take the bull by the horns. We have managed to talk the whole staff into, at least, listening to our ideas and, if we are lucky, they will agree to explore the possibilities of making some changes in the way we assess.

Kay

Making Portfolios Matter in a Balanced Learning Program

Almost anyone can keep a "collection" of their work. While some might call this a portfolio, it is not a portfolio as we define the term.

In our balanced learning program, a portfolio is a special collection of the students' own selections of their best work. Students participate actively in the whole process, making their portfolio folders, identifying the learning criteria and selecting the pieces of their work that demonstrate how they have met the criteria. In addition, reflecting on their work and on the criteria allows students to form new learning goals. In these ways, we use portfolios and make portfolios matter.

What is portfolio assessment?

Portfolio assessment is the process that students go through, from the beginning through to the end of a school year, and from grade to grade, to learn to self-assess and set goals for their learning. The students are active participants in portfolio assessment, selecting samples of their best work to place in their portfolios. Portfolio assessment allows them to critique their own work and to make value judgments. This is important because so many things in life depend upon standards to measure quality. Lumber in a lumberyard meets certain standards. Eggs are graded according to certain standards. Olympic athletes are judged according to certain criteria.

In portfolio assessment, students learn to self-evaluate. The portfolio process gives them essential experience in and opportunities for identifying standards and assessing their own work against specific criteria. If students, from an early age, year after year, learn to participate in determining the criteria that meet high educational standards and to measure their own progress against those standards, they will gain a life skill: self-evaluation.

How do we begin to make students self-evaluators?

In order for students to self-evaluate, they must become skilled critics. The portfolio assessment process involves students in making their own selection of their "best" pieces of work to include in their portfolios. Therefore, students must know and understand the criteria that they will use to assess their work. Traditionally, criteria for assessment and evaluation were "secrets" held only by teachers. However, portfolio assessment requires that students be allowed in on these "secrets" so they can learn to develop their own criteria and to judge their achievements.

According to Bloom's Taxonomy, the highest level of thinking involves generating, holding and applying a set of external and internal criteria. These are the skills that students need in order to become strong self-evaluators. And they are skills that students can be taught. Students, even as early as kindergarten, can begin to learn how to recognize and understand what makes a piece of work "good." Students can learn to react to their own work and to provide insights into their own learning that are increasingly more accurate as the students move along a learning continuum. If students engage in self-evaluation and in monitoring their own growth and progress throughout their school years, they will reach a fairly sophisticated level of competency by the time they graduate.

Portfolio assessment offers the student, teacher and parents evidence of the student's learning. In order to select his or her best piece of work, the student must develop and identify specific learning criteria, produce the evidence of his or her learning (the work sample) and self-assess his or her own work by judging it against the criteria.

A further step in portfolio assessment is for the student to set new learning goals based on his or her progress to date as demonstrated by the samples in the portfolio. This provides a basis that teachers, students and parents can use for discussion and for the development of a plan of action to help the student meet the new learning goals.

Are portfolios an accurate way to evaluate student achievement?

The student portfolio is a major part of the data collection that is integral to a balanced and fair assessment approach in a balanced learning program. The portfolio contains evidence of progress throughout the student's school years, and it is proof of exactly what the student can do. Even if the student does not meet the requirements for a specific grade level, the samples selected for the portfolio always demonstrate advancement. One of the greatest values of the portfolio is that it allows the student to be a stakeholder in the assessment process.

Portfolios need to contain credible evidence of student achievement to be valid assessment tools. Even the most well organized and complete collections will not be accurate or useful for assessment unless they are directly related to curriculum outcomes. The practice of teaching students to construct portfolios is a multifaceted process. It takes time, determination, planning and a sound knowledge base.

Is it possible for a student to have a good portfolio and still be performing below grade level?

A portfolio reflects an individual's personal growth, and it may portray significant improvement in the student's learning during the course of a school year. Despite improvement, the student may still be performing below grade level. Because portfolio assessment is but one component of a balanced assessment program, the teacher is responsible for being honest with parents and students regarding the students' developmental levels and how well they are meeting the expectations for the grade level. The portfolio is one of the most convincing tools that will give hope to struggling students and their parents. It provides concrete evidence that the student is heading toward the desired outcomes, and, through self-evaluation and goal setting, the student is aware of the direction to follow to reach those outcomes.

2

Laying the Groundwork for a Portfolio Program

We, as teachers, make judgments about students
all the time. Since these judgments are based on criteria,
whether we can articulate them or not, we have only
two choices: we can either make our criteria crystal clear
to students or make them guess.

– Judy Arter

January 25. Today we had our first staff session on assessment. We are in the on-going battle of 'coming in line with each other.' We decided to look at student writing as the starting point for inclusion in a portfolio. Teachers brought samples of what they considered excellent, good and weak writing from their classes. Kay and I, as facilitators, made overheads of each and we led a discussion about each sample. There are so many factors to consider and we had heated arguments about what seems like the smallest matters. Our expectations are so very different and the criteria we each use appear to be hit or miss. It was an eye-opener for us all. At least we are familiar enough with each other to argue and that is the first step to some kind of collaboration.

Shirley-Dale

Establishing the Background for a Successful Portfolio Program

There are several steps involved in establishing a portfolio program. While a portfolio is often a whole-school initiative, in some schools only one or two teachers are involved. This often raises some concerns for those teachers, who may feel frustrated and isolated as they try to set up a solid and balanced program that includes portfolios.

In this chapter, we review the basic steps for establishing the right background for a portfolio program. This includes the theoretical and pedagogical issues, as well as some suggestions about what to do in the classroom. We also address some of the common concerns that arise when a school, teams of teachers or individual teachers first begin to implement a portfolio program.

Common Concerns in Creating and Establishing a Portfolio Program

Must all teachers on a staff begin an initiative, such as a portfolio program, at the same time?

It is not necessary and, at times, not even feasible, for all teachers on a staff to begin an initiative simultaneously. It is extremely important for a staff to share the same philosophy of how students learn, supported by current research, but the timing of the implementation of a project based on that philosophy depends upon a variety of factors. Some teachers are greater risk-takers than others. They may make mistakes in their initial attempts, but they use them as learning experiences. Other teachers proceed with more caution, needing additional time to read, reflect, organize and plan before they begin. Nothing was ever gained by undue haste or by forcing teachers to begin an initiative before they are sufficiently prepared. If the initiative is a whole-staff or team approach, it is important that each member be heading in the same direction, regardless of the stage of implementation.

Can an individual teacher without the support of the whole staff successfully implement a new initiative such as portfolio assessment?

Many whole-school initiatives begin with one or two teachers who have exhaustively studied a specific subject or concept and have a strong belief in it. Those teachers take the first steps toward its implementation, and their results can encourage other teachers to participate. The excitement becomes contagious and the work of that small group becomes the model for many teachers. Sometimes there is a "pebble in a pond effect," and the circle of participants becomes increasingly larger and inspires other teachers on staff to learn and follow.

Where can a teacher who is working alone on implementing a portfolio program find support?

If a teacher is working in isolation to initiate a new project at his or her school, there are a variety of possible support resources. These include:

- finding a colleague in another school to share ideas
- professional networking
- visiting classrooms where the practice has been implemented
- researching on the Internet
- video recordings
- enrolling in a university class
- forming a support group in the area
- contacting an expert
- reading educational literature
- attending a national conference

June 10. This has been quite a year! As a staff, we've never been so far apart and we've never been closer. We have thrashed out this portfolio assessment idea for most of the last term. We agreed and we disagreed. There were times when we felt like scrapping it all, but then a break-through, a revelation, and we'd meet again and make great headway. We are still not in complete agreement about a lot of the fine points, but we have agreed on the major concept, we've studied the literature and it looks like we'll be ready to give it a try in September.

Kay

September 4. It is going to be a challenge to guide every student in making his or her own portfolio. I know the important thing is to try not to do too much this first year. I will begin by collecting a few samples. I will collect the first piece of work the students do in their Reading Response Journals, something in Math from their Learning Logs, and something in Science. When I think of the word "baseline," I think of it being associated with the tests I have had concerning my health. I remember when I had my first mammogram; the technician said it was a "baseline." My students' first pieces of work will be included as the baselines in their portfolios.

Kay

What is the first step in a portfolio program at the beginning of the school year?

During the first few weeks of the new school year, the teacher's key objective is to collect the students' first piece of work in each subject that will be included in the portfolios. The teacher should note that the beginning of the year is the only time during the portfolio assessment process that the students themselves are not involved in collecting evidence of their efforts. These teacher-chosen samples are called baseline samples. This is an essential step in the process, as individual students will use their baseline samples to measure growth at a later date.

The students do not need an in-depth explanation of the whole portfolio assessment process at this time. The process can be explained more effectively later on when students become actively involved in constructing their own portfolios closer to the first reporting period.

Important Note: If a portfolio program is a brand new initiative for a school, it is important that everyone involved review and agree on the curriculum, learning criteria and benchmarks that will be used to assess the students. When everyone is working with the same set of expectations, the first step, collecting the baseline samples, can begin.

September 14. I am in the process of collecting their baseline samples. I know that these samples must be true pictures of what they can do at the beginning of the term and I am not to tamper with them in any way. I am not to point out errors and this isn't the time for conferencing with them. I realize that summer takes its toll on learning, and students are often working below their end-of-year level for the previous year, but it has taken everything in my power to collect these samples without interfering. I see so many things that they should be able to do better, but if I correct them or help them correct their errors, I am missing the whole point.

Shirley-Dale

What does the teacher collect as baseline samples?

The teacher needs to determine in advance what assignments will be used as the baseline sample in each subject. For example, in science, the baseline sample might be the first entry in the students' learning log or science journal, and for the spelling baseline, the teacher might dictate a few sentences representing a variety of spelling strategies. To be valid, the samples cannot be revised in any way or corrected by the teacher. However, the students may proofread the samples.

Have students write on looseleaf paper during the first week of school to make it easier to collect the baseline samples.

25

The baseline samples in each subject represent the starting point for the assessment of each student. Reviewing these samples provides the teacher with a quick and concrete overview of the students' developmental levels at the beginning of the school year. There is often a wide range of ability and understanding within a class. The curriculum outcomes and the indicators for developmental levels of learning should guide the teacher in planning instruction, and the baseline samples are invaluable tools in providing direction for that instruction.

From the Files

Using Baseline Samples

Baseline samples represent a starting point for evaluating the progress and achievement of each individual student. One class will probably have students at several developmental levels, as illustrated by the following samples of writing.

Sept 13

Our Tree
I like roots
I like bork
I like onchor tree
I like bronches
I like water
I like food
I like twigs
I like leaves
I like green
I like red

Baseline sample from a grade 2 science class. The students were asked to write a report on their adopted tree. They had brainstormed the words referring to trees on chart paper and that chart was displayed in the classroom. This student merely copied the words from the chart to fill up the page and is at an early stage of writing.

Sept. 13

Our Tree
Our tree has brown and red bark. It looks like it's older than me. It has a very rough bark. The leaves mostley look like ovals. It chages clour in fall. Some parts of the tree is curved. The buds turn into leaves. The roots grow under gound. The tree stores the food in the trunk.

This is a sample collected from another student in the same class. This student is clearly at a more advanced level of writing than the first student.

These are baseline samples of mathematics writing by grade 5 students in the same classroom. The students have been asked to explain their understanding of fractions.

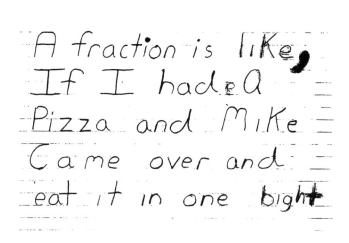

A fraction is like,
If I had a
Pizza and Mike
came over and
eat it in one bight

This student either does not have a good understanding of fractions or cannot express it in writing.

This student demonstrates a clear understanding of the concept.

Constructing Criteria Charts: What the Teacher Needs to Know

What is the first step in teaching students how to self-evaluate?

Teaching students how to self-evaluate needs to start early in the school year. The process begins with teaching the students how to construct class-made criteria charts. Before students can produce competent work, they need to have a clear vision or mental picture of what "competent work" looks like. The teacher's role is to guide the students in discovering the criteria for competent work at any grade level.

How do you construct a class-made criteria chart?

A class-made criteria chart is developed by having the students examine and discuss examples of competent work. The students identify the characteristics that make a piece of work in a given subject area competent. As students learn new concepts and skills during the year, they also revise or add to the criteria charts as necessary. The same basic procedure can be used to develop the criteria chart in any area of study.

It is essential for students to see exemplars, or "direct models," of competent work that fulfill the criteria in a given subject or for a specific task. (The teacher needs to provide a variety of model samples for each subject many times during the year.) When teachers teach concepts, models or exemplars of competent work, and elicit responses and observations from the students, they are helping the students to construct a criteria chart. For example, students will begin to recognize the characteristics of good writing by reading, examining and discussing various pieces of competent writing. The students internalize this knowledge in order to self-evaluate. It also helps them become consistent when judging their own work.

The criteria charts are important tools for students to use on a day-to-day basis. By the time students begin working on their portfolios during the first reporting period, they will be familiar with the points on the criteria charts and will be able to use them with confidence. Teaching students to make criteria charts takes time, but it is time well spent. Periodically, additions or revisions will be made to the chart as new concepts are taught.

As a class, the students and teacher examine an exemplar and discuss the characteristics that make it competent work. Eliciting student responses about these characteristics is important. The teacher records the student responses, using their own words. Criteria charts in most classrooms in a given subject at a given grade will have the same general points. However, using the exact words that the students used will make the criteria chart clearer and more meaningful to the students. The criteria charts provide the students with a common vocabulary to discuss and evaluate their learning in general and specific terms.

Criteria charts should be displayed all year so that students can refer to them while they work and when they are selecting pieces to put in their portfolios. The teacher should encourage students to refer to the charts whenever they check or revise their work to make sure it is complete and fulfills the criteria.

Quick Tip

Refer to the criteria charts on a daily basis, so that students become familiar with the procedure for developing them and get used to using them to critique their own work in progress.

Good Writers Chart — Grade 2	**Good Writers Chart — Grade 7**
1. Make a list of things to write about.	1. Know how to write in different genres.
2. Think about who will read your work.	2. Know how to write the form for different purposes.
3. Your writing must make sense.	3. Research when writing information-type genres.
4. Your writing must have a beginning, middle and end.	4. Organize paragraphs.
5. Put feeling into your writing (sad, happy, angry, excited, surprised).	5. Use vivid images.
6. Put periods, question marks and exclamation marks at the end of your sentences.	6. Use correct vocabulary for the genre.
7. Begin every sentence with a capital. Names of places, names of people and the word "I" need capitals.	7. Use correct spelling and punctuation.
8. Use your best spelling.	8. Use the dictionary and thesaurus.
9. Use detail in your work.	9. Reread and revise.
10. Don't start all your sentences the same.	10. Know how to include dialogue.
11. Proofread your writing.	11. Know how to write in the first person and the third person.
12. Use the thesaurus.	12. Have a personal style.

A grade 2 class-made criteria chart for writing.

A grade 7 class-made criteria chart for writing. In both classrooms, during the first writing lesson, the class supplied four or five points for the charts. New points were added in future lessons. These charts use the students' own words.

What if the students don't come up with some of the most important characteristics?

Many of the points on a criteria chart come from the prior knowledge that students have about a subject, skill or concept. If the students do not suggest important criteria or characteristics themselves, the teacher must find out if the students actually know and can apply the concepts and skills, but didn't think to mention them, or if this is a gap in their learning experiences. The teacher can use questions or examples with the students to elicit this information. If the students do not know and understand important specific characteristics, the teacher must treat these as new concepts and skills for the class to learn, and then address them in specific lessons. This is not a problem in terms of developing the criteria charts since constructing the charts is an on-going process throughout the school year. The charts will be amended and expanded as the students' learning influences what they should be able to achieve.

Before a new characteristic is added to the chart, the students must learn the new concept and see several models of competent work that exemplify it. The teacher and the students should look at and discuss models of new characteristics in the same way that is outlined for developing the initial criteria charts.

Constructing a Criteria Chart

1. Prepare an exemplar, or "direct model," of competent work to place on an overhead, chart paper or the chalkboard.
2. Examine and discuss the characteristics of the exemplar with the class. Elicit from the students the criteria that make the example "good" or competent.
3. Record the students' responses on a class chart, using their own words.
4. Provide many models of good work during the year, and update the chart as necessary.

November 4. Kay and I spent a few minutes after school last week looking at the Writing Criteria Charts in each classroom. We were surprised that they were so similar. The students had come up with almost the same points in almost the same words. This is distressing because, in some cases, they are two or three grades apart. I am finding, also, that most of my students do look up at the chart when they are proofing and revising their writing, but the quality of the writing has not changed significantly. What am I missing? When working on a Provincial Assessment team in the summer, we used exemplars and a standard marking criteria to raise our expectations. I am going to try to follow the same procedure with my class.

Shirley-Dale

What background information does the teacher need in order to guide the students in constructing criteria charts?

One can easily imagine how a brand new grade 7 teacher might feel when faced with the challenge of constructing criteria charts. Perhaps this teacher teaches language arts, and she has collected the baseline writing samples from all the students. She now needs to construct the criteria chart with the class. She might ask herself, "How many of the students are working at grade level? What are the expectations for grade 7 students? How can I help the students advance at their own level? What does competent grade 7 writing look like?" Being able to answer questions like these is a key to making good criteria charts.

One of the first things a teacher should know is how various assessment-related terms are used within his or her board and by colleagues. If teachers do not use the same terminology in the same way, it can produce considerable confusion regarding the different expectations of different teachers. Using the same terms helps teachers to recognize and assess competent work consistently.

Assessment Terminology

benchmark – a standard or reference against which something is measured or evaluated. David Jackson (1983) used the term "benchmarks" to describe specific indicators of what students can generally do at a certain age.

rubric – "a scoring tool that lists the criteria for a piece of work, or 'what counts'" (Heidi Goodrich, 1997). A rubric specifies criteria that indicate several levels of performance.

exemplar – a model or a pattern that meets specific criteria of a good piece of work or a good performance. An exemplar is provided so that the criteria can be copied or imitated.

criteria chart – a list of points extracted from the highest level of proficiency on a rubric. It is used to identify the characteristics of good work.

The teacher must also know and understand the content, concepts and skills in a subject area as set out by the curriculum. For example, in language arts, the teacher's knowledge and understanding of the rudiments of good writing are fundamental. The language arts teacher also needs to know the structures and features of different genres of writing. Teachers can find out what subject-related knowledge and skills they require by studying the curriculum documents, by keeping abreast of the latest research and through collaboration with other educators. This approach to determining the content and skills makes the teacher better equipped to lead the students toward high-level critical observations about what they are studying and how to assess their own learning.

Many school boards and regional departments of education have drawn up explicit and detailed rubrics in various curriculum areas as guidelines for teachers. They may also provide exemplars of student work at several levels of proficiency for each grade level. The exemplars act as benchmarks, or points of reference, for the teacher in measuring each student's performance. Knowing and understanding the rubrics, and studying the exemplars, makes the teacher adept at guiding students in constructing class-made criteria charts.

If there are no such guidelines for the teacher to follow, groups of teachers on the same school staff will need to collaborate to produce a rubric that specifically states the criteria for levels of quality in a specific area of study and, perhaps, spanning a number of grade levels.

When the teacher has internalized the curriculum requirements and the relevant standards for assessment, he or she is ready to work on the criteria charts with the students.

> **Constructing a Rubric**
>
> 1. Gather a group of interested teachers and share recent literature pertaining to rubrics.
> 2. Choose a subject. Teachers in this group collect samples of work that represent weak, acceptable, and superior levels in that subject.
> 3. Distribute copies of the samples or display them on overhead transparencies so the group of teachers can review them together. (This should be done grade by grade.)
> 4. Examine *several* samples at the same level for each grade, assessing each one individually. Identify the characteristics that pertain to the level of each sample. Discuss these openly, and be prepared for debate. Everyone must agree on the characteristics for each level in each grade.
> 5. Place the samples in folders marked "weak," "acceptable," or "superior."
> 6. Clarify and list the characteristics for the samples, according to their grade and level.
> 7. Draft a rubric, and meet again to revise and finalize it.

September 23. Well, I finished the first step and I am so pleased that I actually got the baseline samples collected. I am surprised that it was so easy. Basically, I just took the first pieces of work my students completed. They used large pieces of construction paper and designed the covers of their folders in an art class. We then placed their samples in the folders and put them in a file. I am feeling more relaxed about it. I think we are going to have a few minutes at the end of our next staff meeting to share our experiences. It will be interesting to see how the other teachers made out.

Kay

3

Developing Your Portfolio Program

There is nothing noble in being superior
to some other person. True nobility is
being superior to your previous self.
– Middle School Document

*November 14. Report cards go out in a week and a half and I know I have
a lot of work to do. I have been thinking for weeks about how I am going to
introduce the portfolio idea to my class. I know I can't expect the class to
know how to make a portfolio or even what it is. You can't just say, for
example, 'knit me a sweater' and expect me to know how to knit a sweater.
I had a brain wave. I decided to have an artist friend of mine visit the class
with his portfolio. After seeing Steve's portfolio and hearing him explain to
the class why he chose each piece, they can hardly wait to get started on
their own.*

Kay

The Difference Between Portfolios and Work Files

A work file and a portfolio are not the same thing, although both contain pieces of
student work. A work file is simply a collection of a student's work. In contrast, a
portfolio is a refined selection of student work. A portfolio houses student-chosen
samples of the student's best work. These samples are used as evidence of the student's highest achievement. A portfolio is not only a storage unit, but is part of an
assessment process that teaches students to evaluate and present their own work.

Students compare and evaluate the samples with their previous work and use
them to identify new learning goals. In participating in portfolio assessment, students are involved in a process that tracks their progress over time and helps them
to get to know themselves as learners. The process is just as important as the end
product.

The contents of the working portfolio guide and inform instructional decisions
throughout the year. It is a formative assessment for the student and the teacher.
The cumulative portfolio is, basically, a report card for the teacher. It is an evaluation of the effectiveness of the teaching that occurred in the classroom. It is the
summative assessment for both the teacher and the student. The cumulative portfolio will be an invaluable assessment tool for guiding and informing instructional
decisions in the next year.

What are the components of a portfolio?

The portfolios that students construct in our portfolio program have two sections and each one serves a specific purpose.

The Working Portfolio – The working portfolio contains the students' work samples; that is, the baseline samples and the students' "best work samples" from the first and second reporting periods. The final school term's work is placed in the cumulative portfolio. The working portfolio is sent home with the students at the end of the school year.

Baseline Samples – The teacher collects the first piece of work the students produce in the first few weeks of the new school year. These samples are called the baseline samples and will be used to measure growth or improvement in the students' work when compared to the samples collected in the first reporting period. These samples are dated and stored in the working portfolio until the first reporting period.

First Reporting Period Samples – The students select their best samples for this reporting period from the work accumulated throughout the term, following a set criteria. They compare these particular pieces of work with their baseline samples, write an explanation of why they chose them and set goals for the next term. These samples are dated and stored in the working portfolio until the second reporting period.

Second Reporting Period Samples – Students follow the same procedure as they do in the first reporting period. Using Criteria Charts, they choose their best work, compare them with the first term samples, reflect on their own achievements and set goals for the final term. These samples are dated and stored in the working portfolio until the final reporting period.

The Cumulative Portfolio – The cumulative portfolio contains the students' end-of-year samples from the work accumulated during the last term of the school year. The cumulative portfolio is the collection of the students' "end-of-year" samples, except students are comparing their second term selections with their final term samples. Reflections and goals for the next year accompany each piece.

The cumulative portfolio is passed on to the new teacher in the new school year. This provides continuity in learning from one grade to the next.

How do you go from a collection of work to a portfolio?

To go from a simple collection of work to a portfolio, the teacher needs to understand and use the components in a portfolio. Our students maintain sets of files for everyday work, including their writing files, learning logs, and notebooks. They use these everyday files as the source from which they choose their best work during a reporting period.

Our student portfolios have two sections: the "working portfolio" and the "cumulative portfolio." The working portfolio contains the most recent assessment "evidence" for each student. Each reporting period has its own separate folder (coded by color), and the best work from a given reporting period is stored in its appropriate folder.

The "cumulative portfolio" is where the students keep their best pieces of work from the last reporting period of the school year. The cumulative portfolio follows the student from year to year and grade to grade.

The first items to be placed in the working portfolio are the baseline samples obtained at the beginning of school year. (Again, the baseline samples are the *only* pieces of work that are *not* selected by the students.) For the first reporting period, the students select their best work from their everyday work files to place in the first reporting period folder. The students compare their pieces of work with the criteria charts and the baseline samples. They evaluate their best work sample and develop new learning goals. The baseline and first reporting samples are put in their respective folders, which are then placed in the working portfolio. This process is repeated at the end of each reporting period, with the students using their samples to measure their growth and/or improvement since the previous reporting period.

Introducing the Portfolio Program to Students

When and how do you explain the portfolio program to the students?

Near the end of the first term, the teacher needs to introduce the concept of keeping a portfolio (or to refresh students' memories if they are already familiar with the portfolio assessment process). *Preparing a Piece of Work for Your Portfolio* on page 39 can be distributed to students to help them understand the process.

Students will need to go through this whole process a few times. The teacher should have a variety of baseline and first reporting samples for the class to work with. After the first demonstration by the teacher, the students should contribute their own ideas and compare the samples, using the class-made criteria chart. Their comments should be noted under the appropriate heading. (Note: Students should address each heading separately.)

When the students have had some practice, they can use their own, real baseline samples, which were collected at the beginning of the school year. The teacher can move from student to student, facilitating them in the process of self-evaluation and goal setting. As the students work independently, the teacher and other classroom helpers can move around the classroom, giving help and encouragement when needed. The working portfolios are then collected and stored.

How important is the student's choice of "best work" in the portfolio process?

In the past, all students were given a mark only at the end of a unit or section of work. In some cases, students were marked on every single assignment and the mark was averaged at the end of the term. There were no opportunities for them to practice or to learn from their mistakes. Marking was somewhat of a mystery to students and something to fear. The student had no input or feedback from the mark. It was a secret that only teachers knew and they had no part in the whole process.

When students select their own best work for their portfolios, they are identifying their own strengths and writing about them. This is a tremendous confidence builder. There is a positive impact on students as they identify their weaknesses as goals. Now, instead of the teacher pointing out their mistakes, the students are responsible for recognizing them and for searching for ways they can improve. There is concrete evidence of their success. The teacher and the student now share the responsibility of assessment.

Quick Tip

When students prepare their reflections and goals, it is important not to restrict the amount of space students have for their answers. A reproducible sheet with preset headings and a space for responses can limit the amount the student will write, and it tends to restrict their thought process as well.

Quick Tip

Many teachers often assume that students automatically understand the concept of setting goals. In reality, many students have heard the word "goal," but they may never have thought of what it means in relation to their work. Setting goals is a skill that must be taught, modeled, and practiced just like any other concept. Students usually associate "goal" to its meaning in hockey or soccer. This is an ideal way to bring meaning to the concept of goals. The teacher can then present the dictionary definition "the result toward which effort is directed," and help students to see how setting goals applies to their own learning.

Portfolio Procedure for Teachers

1. Motivate the students. Have students prepare first reporting period folder as detailed in Suggested Materials to Assemble on page 46.

2. Find a sample of student writing at grade level produced early in the school year. Find a second sample produced by the same student during the latter part of the first reporting period. Label these as "baseline sample" and "first reporting period sample."

3. Make an overhead transparency with both the baseline sample and the first reporting period sample on the same sheet.

4. Write headings, "Why I Chose This Piece" and "Goals for Next Term" on chart paper or the chalk board.

5. Model the procedure the students will follow by comparing the samples and reflecting aloud, using the points on the class-made criteria chart for good writing.

6. Record the thoughts under the heading "Why I Chose This Piece" on the chalkboard or chart paper, noting growth and progression between the two.

7. Examine the first reporting period sample again, using the class-made criteria chart to identify areas that need improvement.

8. Write those points under the heading "Goals for Next Term."

9. Repeat the procedure with other baseline samples and first reporting period samples. This time, the students contribute their ideas, comparing the samples using the class-made criteria chart. The teacher records their observations on chart paper under the heading, "Why I Chose This Piece."

10. "Goals for Next Term" are elicited from the students and recorded on chart paper or the chalk-board.

11. Give the students their baseline samples. These were collected and stored at the beginning of the school year.

12. Circulate around the classroom facilitating students in the process of self-evaluation and goal setting.

Preparing a Piece of Work for Your Portfolio

✓   **Check off each step as you complete it.**

___1. Find your collection of work for _____(subject) of this reporting period. Bring your work to your desk or table.

___2. Write your name and the date in the top right corner of a sheet of paper. Write the heading "Why I Chose This Piece" at the top of the page.

___3. Examine your work carefully. Use the points on the class-made criteria chart to help you choose the best piece of work for the subject.

___4. Put the baseline or works sample from the last reporting period beside the piece of work you chose. Refer to the criteria chart and compare your new piece of work to the other piece of work. Look for growth and improvement in your new piece.

___5. Identify your own strengths as you reflect on your new piece of work. Write them down under the heading "Why I Chose This Piece."

___6. Take a new sheet of paper and write "Goals For Next Term" at the top of the page. Identify areas in your new piece of work that need improvement and write them down under "Goals for Next Term."

___7. Attach the pages with your reflections and goals to the new sample of work you chose.

___8. Place the baseline sample in the baseline folder and your sample of work from the reporting period in its reporting period folder. Place both of these folders in your working portfolio.

March 20. Portfolios were on the staff meeting agenda again this month. We are trying to iron out all of our questions and concerns. It seems that the more we know the more we don't know. The big debate this time was about whether or not the students should have the freedom to choose what they think is best. We are finding it so hard to give up the reins. Some of us were able to let them have equal status, but the loudest voices came from the others: "I am the teacher, after all. I'd be shirking my responsibility if I turned over the responsibility to my students." "I've already marked the work and had them make the corrections, is this the work I use?" " I just can't let them put in work that has errors in it. They know better." The teachers who put the work in the portfolios for the students spent hours and hours selecting from the mounds of student work-files, notebooks and binders. They are the ones who are questioning the worth of portfolios. I guess we really are like the students in our classrooms, all at various levels of learning.

Shirley-Dale

What should the teacher do if he or she disagrees with the student's choice?

This is one of the most difficult issues for teachers who have been accustomed to being the sole evaluator in the classroom. The point is that if a student does choose an inferior piece of work as the best effort, he or she lacks understanding of the characteristics of competent work. This is often an eye-opener for the teacher and a good assessment tool in itself. It is important that the teacher respect the student's choice, but the teacher should recognize it as an indication that he or she must give more help to that student. There are always students who need remedial help or a little push to achieve their best results.

If the teacher disagrees with selections made by some students and believes that it is not representative of their best work, he or she may want to put a better piece in the portfolio. However, this should be discussed with the student and a note should accompany the sample, indicating that it was teacher-chosen and why it was chosen. The student's choice must stay in the portfolio as well.

Should a teacher place items in a student's portfolio?

This question has caused some debate among educators. Some feel that adding teachers' samples would take away the ownership of the portfolio. It would no longer totally belong to the student. To include teacher-chosen samples ultimately would be the decision of the teacher. Some teachers may feel strongly that what the student has selected does not present the full picture of what the student can do. If teacher-chosen samples of student work are included, they should be clearly marked "teacher chosen" or a "T" printed at the top. The teacher should include the reason why that particular sample was chosen.

Other items included by the teacher may be tests, interviews, surveys, anecdotal records, checklists, and developmental continua in various subjects. If teachers include a test, it may be wise to examine why it should be included and what the test evaluates. Is it representative of what the students really know, and is it enriching the portfolio? Tests are primarily used to evaluate, to judge at the end of a unit, term or year whether or not students understand what has been taught. A high-quality test will measure what the students really understand about concept and content, not just what is easy to measure.

October 12. We had a staff meeting and it looks like we have a full school collection of baseline samples. Some teachers seem more excited and interested than others. The question arose, "What do we do next?" We are aware that the students have to be involved before the next reporting period. They will be the ones choosing the samples of work. They will be the ones who make the decisions about what is their best work. This much we do know, but how do we get to that point?

Shirley-Dale

What should the samples of work "look" like?

The quality of the samples collected will always be influenced by the quality of the teaching. The teacher must teach new concepts and skills to the students so that the students can incorporate the new learning in their work. The teacher and students revise the criteria charts when necessary. It should be noted that the students themselves become more responsible for their own learning when they are able to construct criteria charts. The process gives them greater insight into what makes their work competent, superior or inferior when judged against the criteria. This is demonstrated in the students' work habits and work products, and especially in the depth of the reflective thinking the student does in evaluating why they chose the piece of work and what their new learning goals are.

Teachers should look for comments in "Why I Chose This Piece of Work" that indicate the students' ability to identify the criteria that have been met. This shows that the student is aware of and can integrate the skills and concepts that match those criteria. When the student develops new learning goals, he or is she is identifying what skills and concepts are still lacking in a piece of work.

Student Reflections on Their Own Learning

The following writing samples reflect meaningful, relevant learning, which the students experienced in interactive classrooms. The student-chosen writing samples are supported by the students' reflections on their work.

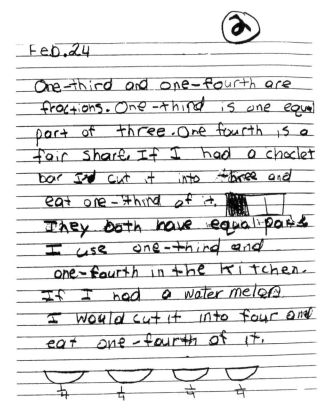

This sample of math writing by a grade 2 student defines the concept of fractions and relates it to a real-life experience. In the reflection, the student recognizes points that are essential for good math writing.

Feb. 24

One-third and one-fourth are fractions. One-third is one equal part of three. One fourth is a fair share. If I had a choclet bar I'd cut it into three and eat one-third of it. They both have equal parts. I use one-third and one-fourth in the kitchen. If I had a water melon I would cut it into four and eat one-fourth of it.

Mar 23 Why is This My Best?

This is my best work because I used capitals and punction marks. It is complete and it is my best spelling. I used Mathematical language. My work is correct.

This reading response shows that the student has internalized the author's message and has been able to express her own reactions to the poem, relating it to her own feelings. It is evident that she has been taught to respond at a critical/evaluative level in the classroom.

"Black River" .... I felt that 'Black River' was a very well written poem. When the author David McCord writes about how the air bites his lungs I feel a cold chill run through my body. When the sled goes down the hill and the high pressured wind slows, I begin to feel warmer like I'm there and the powerful wind stops eating at my face.

I feel I am the one with the frozen tears on my face, I am the one who will run up the hill next.

When David McCord said "I lie there in a deep sleep, every muscle in my body gives a last grind and drops like a wet rag." I can picture everything. A cold boy, laying at the bottom of the hill almost stunned. Then he decides to get back up, to go for it again. Like a whole new life, a new growth of energy.

When I slide down a steep hill, on a cold frosty day, I somewhat share the same experience. Sliding down, and then hopping up to go again, sliding .... again and again until its time to go.

March 17,

I chose this piece of writing "Black River, because I think I wrote and understood what the author, David McCord, was trying to give.

I knew what the story was about and I somewhat have shared the same experiences.

I know this is a free verse' and I also enjoy writing this genre of liteture.

Is there a safe place on earth?

Their is no place where nothing can happen if you live in Hawaii you are on a volcano itself. If you live in the desert you could get a massive sandstorm if you live near a big river you are in a flooding position.

You have to live by a river to get water so automatically you are in trouble.

You have to live in one place or another and everyplace has it's own natural hazard Flooding, earthquake, tornado volcano blizzard, ICE STORM, etc. In Canada you get snows that could lead to icestorms in USA Is very hot, you could get tornado's volcano's earthquakes, floods, if you live in Asia you could get massive sandstorms.

I think between NB and Australia there is no safer place

I chose these pieces because they are some of my best pieces of writing.
My "Is There A Safe Place On Earth" piece I have good paragraphing, descriptive language and took a while to write. It was well written I had my ideas right and put alot of effort in writing it.

It was a page long and approved by the teacher.

The social studies writing sample shows that the student has a knowledge of natural disasters and an ability to make an evaluative statement based on that

Realistic Fiction													
Historical Fiction													
Folklore													
Fantasy													
Science Fiction													
Poetry													
Informational													
Biography													

This is a reading graph made by a grade 3 student for her portfolio. This is an indication of the genres of literature she has been reading this term and she includes her goals.

Reading Goals
Read more Biography, Science-Fiction, Informational, Poetry, Folklore and Historical

Date March 21st

Nov 23

Why I Chose this work

I chose this work because
it longer than Septenbers
work this work was interestion
and my best work.
My October work had five
more lines

Why I Chose This Personal
Recount

I chose this recount because I
proof read my work. I cheeked
for spelling mistakes, capitals, and
punctuation. I used as much detail
as I could and I made sure
it made sense. When I proofread my
work I go along every line
and see if I need to cheak
for mistakes June 17/

These reflections represent the growth of one student in the ability to interpret and apply the points on the writing criteria chart from the first reporting period in grade 2 to the end of the school year.

The following samples show not only achievement, but growth and progress over a period of time. It is an indication that the students have been taught to write in many genres across the curriculum.

DER MOM
MY SHOES
R
LOVE SMLL
LINDSAY

APR 8

i LiKe THe
PAhT WAHe
SHe ATe
THe BUG!

Reading Response
Oct.

These samples show growth over a period of two years. A Kindergarten student near the end of the second term wrote the "Letter to Mom." "Bug" was written by the same student during the first reporting period of Grade 1 and "Turtle" was the selection chosen by the student for the cumulative portfolio.

1. Turtles   are slow.
2. Turtles Can   swm.
3. They live in there Shel.
4. They hide in there Shel.
4. They protecked there Selves by there
                Shel.
5. They eat Plants unden water.
6. They are so Slow because of there
        Shel. bause its So hevy.

                            Grade One

44

Sept. 22

Trees are homes For bruds
and for cats to slep in the shddo.

the trees have roots, bark, leaves, branches,
trunk

The teacher chose the selection about trees as a baseline sample. The same student as a first term entry chose "Light." The sample chosen by the student for the cumulative portfolio is entitled "What I Learned About Garter Snakes."

Oct 27

what I Learned About light

I Learned That light can
bos from a mere to mere
and wan you move the
mere you'l see that the
light moves to.

The world gos aronde exve
day and There are a
sun eclipe and there is a
moon eclipe.

April 9
What I learnes adout
Garter Snakes I learned
that Garter Snakes have 3 stipes
theit go down their backs
They have 300 pairs of rib
going down its body and
they can eot something 3
times the sise of its head.
I also learned that they
expqnd and contrast
their mucles like an accandian
They are rephtles and
their skin is dry and smooth
not slimy. Their skin is
made out of the same
stuff as our fingernails.

Materials, Time, and Storage: Important Considerations

What materials does the teacher need to gather to organize, construct and store portfolios?

The ability to organize materials is one of the most important elements in portfolio assessment. The teacher will need a variety of supplies, ranging from construction paper and file folders to class lists and rubrics. A computer or an audiotape player/recorder may even be required. It is essential for the teacher to develop an efficient system to help both students and teacher construct, organize and store the students' work because a tool that is cumbersome, time-consuming and hard to access will not be used.

Materials and Equipment for Constructing Portfolios

Assessment-Related Items

– copies of class lists
– rubrics (if available — regional, local, school, class)
– observational notebooks
– survey/interview forms
– curriculum outcomes for the grade level and/or subject
– exemplars of competent work for the subject and grade level

Stationery Supplies for Portfolio Construction

– file folders (class sets of regular and hanging folders in four different colors)
– labels
– paper
– construction paper
– chart paper
– markers, pens, pencils, crayons
– scissors
– tape and glue

Storage

– boxes that accommodate hanging files (durable plastic bins work well)

Equipment/Hardware

– depending on what the teacher includes in the portfolios, additional items such as
  – audio tapes, tape recorder
  – computer, scanner, CD-burner, computer disks/ CD-ROMs (other computer storage devices and accessories)
  – camera and/or digital camera and/or video camera

An efficient portfolio assessment system allows both the teacher and the students quick and easy access to the pieces of work. A color-coding system works well for this, especially for younger children. The teacher might have all the students in the class take a large sheet of red construction paper and make a folder for the baseline samples. Students place their names, the date and the year on the front of the folders and then decorate them to stress ownership. A table of contents is placed on the left inside cover of the folder. Students number each sample, matching the samples to the items listed in the table of contents. This red folder, containing the baseline samples, is placed in a file folder that is called the "working portfolio." The working portfolio is stored until the first reporting period. (In our school, there are four times during the school year when samples of work will be placed in the portfolio: at the beginning of the school year, and at the end of the first, second and final reporting periods.) To prevent confusion and to make it easier to access the files, students can use a different color for each reporting period file.

The teacher can add another dimension to the assessment evidence in the portfolio by recording the students' reading proficiency on audiotape. The teacher records the student reading at the beginning of the first school term and compares that reading with the second term recording. This is an excellent method of measuring reading ability and of tracking the student's progress and growth. The same tape should follow the student throughout their elementary years.

Keeping recordings on audiotape also raises the question of equipment and additional storage needs for portfolios. The teacher and students must have access to a good tape recorder that produces a clear recording. As well, a machine that plays back the sound well is needed during the conferencing part of portfolio assessment. Each recorded reading needs to be logged by date, purpose, etc. The individual tapes should be labeled with this information as well.

Quick Tip

A digital camera is an invaluable tool in any classroom, but particularly when gathering evidence for a portfolio.

How successful and realistic is it to attempt electronic portfolios?

Electronic portfolios offer portfolio assessment teachers a variety of attractive advantages. Data in digital form can be cross-referenced easily, overlaid and analyzed. With a few keystrokes, teachers, students and parents can compare evidence of a given student's learning on a particular subject over several years. The digital files require less physical space than the actual hard copy items. However, before implementing electronic portfolios with a class, the teacher should consider the following factors:

Access – Both the teacher and students should be able to access the hardware and software. The teacher must make sure there are enough computers, scanners and printers available.

High-End Tools – Depending on the subject matter, multiple data sources (text, video, images, etc.) will need to be stored. Access to at least one high-end workstation with a scanner, OCR (optical character recognition), software, printer and digital camera will be needed.

Computer Memory – Graphics and photographic images take up a great deal more computer system storage than text. Be sure that the school's system can support large files without compromising other applications. Creating back-up files or using CD-ROM storage will help in avoiding an unnecessary drain on the system or the loss of vital material.

Labor – Accumulating information for an electronic portfolio is both labor-intensive and time-consuming.

Administration – A database application is necessary to establish an area for each student, to store various file formats and to allow for annotated comments appended to each item. A security feature with password protection is also required.

March 20. I noticed that two of the students chose pieces of writing that I did not think were really good examples of their best work. As I reflect, I think that they may have chosen them because of the topic, which was hockey. They live and breathe hockey. Or it could be that they just need to see more models of competent work. I think I will review the criteria chart with them during writing workshop. I am not going to ask them to choose

47

again but I think I will ask them if I could choose a sample that represents their best and place it in their portfolio. I will label it as teacher-chosen and write why.

Kay

November 21. In some ways this week was like the blind leading the blind. The students and I are all learning at the same time. But I do have a great sense of accomplishment. I was so glad to have the help of my student intern and our resource teacher or I may not have made it. Some students needed one-on-one assistance for the whole procedure. Others caught on quite quickly. They are all completed and put away.

Kay

How much time should the teacher and students spend on preparing the portfolio?

The portfolio program concept is an integral part of the learning process and is on-going throughout the year. The students are always using the criteria charts for different subjects. The modeling aspect — by the teacher in his or her daily work and through the display of specific exemplars —is also a continuing part of the process.

The process of physically making the portfolio each term can be accomplished in the week before the reporting period by using small blocks of time each day. For example, in mathematics, instead of writing in their learning logs on a particular day, students could examine their entries for the term and identify their best efforts. The next day, the same students might make their selections from their writing folder. The full portfolio, for most students, can be prepared in that one week. A few students might need one-on-one assistance, and time must be allotted for them to prepare their portfolios and to meet with the same success as the rest of the class.

June 10. This week my class completed their portfolios. The procedure went like clockwork this time because they were familiar with the procedure. The more competent students even had time to help the struggling students, saving a lot of time for us all. When they looked at their baseline samples again, there were hoots of laughter at their own mistakes at the beginning of the year. They begged me to let them have "show and tell" so they could share their funniest pieces. It turned out to be a learning experience in itself, even though it was an impromptu plan. Now, they have taken all but the final term samples home. The portfolios in the other grades will be passed on to the next-grade teachers at the end of the year but mine are ready to be sent to the middle school. I do not know the fate of this valuable little carton of portfolios. I am almost possessive of it but I am just going to trust that the whole year's work will not be in vain.

Shirley-Dale

What happens to the portfolios when students move on to middle school and high school?

Ideally, the elementary school portfolios will be passed on to the middle schools and, subsequently, to the high schools. It would give teachers the opportunity to follow the progress of each student over time and to track each student's developmental levels. Strengths and weaknesses could be discerned easily and a continuum of learning for each student would not be disrupted.

Quick Tip

Begin working on cumulative portfolios four to five weeks before the end of the school year to take advantage of the peak learning time for students.

How can middle school teachers accommodate the storage of hundreds of portfolios?

Middle school classroom organization is often different from that in elementary schools. Teachers are responsible for certain subjects, and students move from classroom to classroom throughout the day. A mathematics teacher, for example, may have as many as 120 students from four different classes gathering samples of their best math writing for their portfolios. How does a teacher manage all of these samples? How do they get placed in the students' portfolios? And how does it all fit in with the demands of a busy day?

Middle schools that have the best results have adopted a team approach for portfolio assessment. Teams of teachers meet to organize, plan and implement the process. It is at the early meetings that these team-members must identify the management issues. The initial work may be time-consuming, but the benefits are realized in the end result.

Management Tips for Teams of Teachers

We have culled these tips from our own and other teachers' years of experience in working with teams of teachers to implement a portfolio program.

1. The students' portfolios are stored in the *homeroom* classroom.
2. Each teacher collects baseline samples in only his or her subject area.
3. The students take the baseline samples to their homeroom classrooms and place them in their own portfolios.
4. When samples have been collected from all subjects and placed in the students' working portfolios, they are put in the storage box and put away.
5. At each reporting period, teams of teachers make a schedule of the times they will work on portfolio samples in each subject area. Students will choose their best work in each subject using the criteria charts and write reflections and goals. The timetable should allow for no more than one subject per class per day so as not to overwhelm students.
6. At the beginning of "Portfolio Assessment Week," the homeroom teacher gets out the box and places it in a convenient area in the classroom. Students carry their own working portfolios with them for that week to be used in all subjects. They need their previous term's samples for comparisons, reflections, and goal setting for the next term.
7. Students use their working portfolios for planning, preparing, and conducting student-led conferences.
8. The working portfolios are then placed in the storage box until the next reporting period.

If a school or team of teachers has not identified portfolio assessment as a priority, and a teacher wishes to initiate the process in an individual classroom or subject, the portfolios should be kept in that classroom only.

June 6. Shirley-Dale and I are excited about a call we received from the Department of Education. We have been invited to present a portfolio assessment seminar at the Summer Institute entitled 'Literacy: A Constellation of Strategies.' It will be held on July 12th so we have a lot of work to do. We decided to call it 'The Proof is in the Pudding,' taken directly from the first discussion on the first night when we talked about the need for evidence to accompany report cards.

Kay

The Portfolio in Middle School and High School

Unfortunately, portfolio assessment is not always easily managed in middle and high school. A middle or high school teacher is often responsible for teaching hundreds of students in only one or two subjects. The sheer magnitude of maintaining a portfolio program is often overwhelming.

It is also problematic when some feeder schools send portfolios on to middle and high school, while others do not. However, many teachers in middle and high school have found that portfolio assessment can serve some very useful purposes. Here are few of the things some of these teachers had to say about portfolios and portfolio programs.

Know the underlying pedagogy. It is essential. – Sometimes, a teacher may try portfolio assessment, but meet with little success. It may start to feel like more trouble than it is worth, with the teacher dealing with piles of work samples, but having no time to do anything with them. At times like this, it can be helpful for the teacher to step back and review what he or she knows about the portfolio assessment process. One middle school teacher who was experiencing problems explained that before abandoning portfolio assessment, she decided to read some of the literature about the process. She discovered that she knew very little about it. "I was giving my students no responsibility and was controlling everything myself," she explained. After becoming more informed, she began portfolio assessment the next year with a better background. "I learned that the key to success is knowledge and perseverance, and then more knowledge and more perseverance. Now when I come to a stumbling block, I know how to solve it!"

Use a team approach. – "The idea that two heads are better than one is true. I was fortunate that my team members were all willing to try portfolio assessment," one teacher said. Members of his staff went to a workshop together and that was the springboard for the investigation of portfolio assessment that followed. "The planning stage was the next step. We have been together as a team for three years now and have worked out the major glitches. It takes commitment and patience, but we feel that we have a worthwhile project in place and that it could never have happened without team effort."

Use portfolios in individual subjects. – It is more difficult for teachers who see a group of students for only one or two subjects to maintain the files and portfolio entries than it is for a classroom teacher who teaches all the subjects. If the individual subject teachers want to do portfolio assessment, it is more feasible to use separate portfolios in individual subjects.

One grade 8 math teacher said, "I am the only teacher in my department who is interested in getting my students involved in making portfolios this year. I researched math portfolios on the Internet and extracted ideas from a number of articles until I came up with a suitable model for my classes. This has been a great learning tool for me as it points out what students know and what they don't know. The students are beginning to recognize signs of their own growth and to make judgments about themselves as mathematicians."

Use portfolios with a limited number of students, such as a group of exceptional students. – Limiting the number of students the teacher tracks with a portfolio can allow the teacher to devote the appropriate time, lessons and input to portfolio assessment. A middle school resources teacher used portfolio assessment in the following way.

"I am a middle school resource teacher responsible for exceptional students. At the end of June each year, I make a trip to all of the elementary feeder schools and get a list of the students whom I will be teaching the next year. I gather their portfolios from the classroom teacher, if they are available. These portfolios are clear indicators to me where I should begin my instruction with each student. In the following school year, I continue the process of teaching self-assessment and reflection in my sessions with them. I feel that Middle School is a huge jolt as it is, and I can make it easier for them to adjust if I meet them at their own level and help them follow a continuum of learning."

Use portfolios as a diagnostic tool. – "I do not have time to review the stacks of portfolios that are sent to me from the elementary feeder schools, but I do have time to go to the portfolios and pick out the files for specific students. I have used them for students who are gifted, students who appear to be underachievers, and students who have behavior problems and are not performing at grade level. It would take months for me to discover the previous level of performance without the evidence provided in the portfolios."

4

Deciding What to Put in the Portfolio

Neither teacher nor student can succeed
without a clear vision of what students must
know and be able to do, or without the ability
to translate that vision into actions that result
in high quality work.

– Stiggins

*September 20. Two years have passed, and Shirley-Dale and I are still
giving workshops on Portfolio Assessment. We have been energized by the
teachers' response and excitement. There have been so many questions
asked. This has led us to realize that it's not just a matter of getting
students to make portfolios. It's much deeper than that. There is really no
way to stop the ball from rolling now. Once we got started, we had the
thirst to read everything and to know everything. It's amazing that two
years have slipped by, and we are still changing and learning.*

Kay

*September 30. Another school year is underway and, yesterday, at our staff
meeting, Kay and I were given the floor for a half hour to review portfolio
assessment rationale and the procedure. The new principal, the new
teachers on staff, and the student interns have asked for the full session at
a later date. The question that they asked (one of the most frequently asked
questions in our workshops) was, "What goes in a portfolio?" There are a
lot of questions that radiate from that one, seemingly simple, question.*

Shirley-Dale

Deciding What to Put in the Portfolio

What goes in a portfolio?

The kinds of materials or learning products that are placed in the student portfolio
will vary. The contents could be determined through a school-based decision, a
team decision or the decision of an individual teacher. If the portfolio program is a
school-based project or a team approach, teachers can hold meetings to decide on
the items to be included in the portfolio. In each new school year, meetings should
be held to evaluate the proceedings and progress to date and the changes needed
for future success.

One of the main goals of a portfolio program is to track the progress of students
over time. To measure progress accurately, items of a similar nature have to be

collected at regular intervals. For example, if a reading response is collected as a baseline, the students should be directed to select samples of reading responses in the first, second and final school terms. Each sample will have an attached page of self-reflections and goals written by the student. If a baseline item is collected from a science journal, the science journal should be used again for the ensuing reporting periods. Individual teachers can decide if they want to include additional items relating to their particular curriculum outcomes.

The contents of a portfolio could be an individual teacher's choice if a portfolio program is not a whole-school initiative. In this case, the teacher would examine the curriculum outcomes and choose items accordingly. For example, an elementary teacher, in language arts, might decide to include a written retelling that would help to assess student comprehension of text. In mathematics, the teacher might ask students to choose their best sample from their learning logs, illustrating what they have learned in mathematics that term. In science, a major project may be the end result of a unit, and the teacher might ask students to choose a representation of their best work. A photograph (possibly using a digital camera) of the project accompanied by a written description of what the student learned might be a student's choice for a science sample.

There is really no minimum or maximum number of items in a portfolio. It is more important that each selection is representative of the student's personal best, that it reflects the level of proficiency in specific curriculum outcomes and that it contains the student's self-assessment and goals. The quality of the samples or evidence collected is directly related to the quality of the teaching that takes place in a classroom. Teachers who are continually learning and evaluating their own practices are models for their students. They will be more likely to provide a rich learning environment where inquiry, analysis and questioning are valued, and this will be reflected in the whole portfolio process.

If the teacher knows the curriculum outcomes well, has a clear vision of the end result and high expectations of the students, the portfolio items selected will be more valid as assessment tools. The items chosen will serve to pinpoint the developmental levels of the students in various subjects.

October 18. Today we presented a workshop in a school that has been using portfolio assessment for a few years. They wanted tips and ideas to better their portfolios and to review the process. Staff members brought whole portfolios to the session, and we had a chance to look at them and discuss them. What was in them? Well, some of the portfolios were exceptionally good, showing a lot of thought and innovative ideas. But a couple of them were comprised of the whole writing file for that student for one year; no selections, no reflections, no goals. Others were simply packs of worksheets, stapled together and all marked by the teacher. We talked all the way home about these portfolios reflecting quality. Not so much the quality of the work, but the quality of the teaching that led to that work. Is it the student or the teacher who is being assessed?

Shirley-Dale

Learning from Different Grades

Portfolio items in grades 1–6 – The quality and quantity of the contents placed in a portfolio are influenced and determined by a number of factors. If a teacher or group of teachers is in the beginning stages of implementation, there may be only a few entries or selections. If they are at a more advanced stage of implementation, portfolios may have a wide variety of items from a broad curriculum perspective. The samples here illustrate the variety of items that can be included in student portfolios

from grades 1–6. This extensive table of contents from a cumulative portfolio of the end of grade 2 is an indication that the teacher has been implementing the process of portfolio assessment for several years. For easier access, the number preceding each item corresponds to the number written at the top of the page of each portfolio entry. Items 1–3 are chosen from journals, learning logs and reading response notebooks. Item 4 is a summary of what the student learned at the completion of a science project. Items 5–6 are developmental level checklists charting the progress and stages of learning of the student in mathematics and reading. Item 7 has been selected by the student as the sample that best met the points on the writing criteria chart from the final-term writing folder. Item 8 is a piece of artwork depicting complementary and neutral colors. (Each item, with the exception of the continua charts, is accompanied by student reflections and goals.)

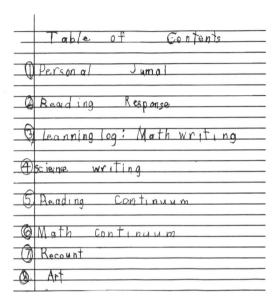

Table of contents from a cumulative portfolio at the end of grade 2

If creativity and higher-level thinking skills are encouraged, the portfolio contents will also contain high-quality selections. For example, one exemplary piece of math writing showing a clear understanding of a concept would far surpass pages of algorithms. Likewise, one cohesive writing sample can outweigh any number of "fill-in-the-blank" sheets.

Portfolio Table of Contents — Grade 6

1. **Reading Response**

2. **Math Explanation**

3. **Newspaper Critique**

4. **Reading Graph**

Table of contents from a cumulative portfolio at the end of grade 6. The teacher, in this case, is in the first year of implementation in portfolio assessment and has focused on four items only.

Home sweet
Dear Home
Diary: 1295 AD

Since I have been in Cathay
I have learned four different
languages and I saw brown
hairy things there called
monkeys. I saw vast castles
I have been through a lot.
Nobody believed me when I got home so I
proved it I undid my coat
and tons of gold fell out.
It looks like I did get
to see the water of Venice again.
By Marco polo

This grade 3 student has been taught and encouraged to write creatively and factually in social studies class.

The Metre

Hello Man! I am here to outline the metre for you. The metre is a new part of the metric system, and is a very prominent part in measurement.

Like most of all the other children you probably play board games, and like most of the other children you probably use a table to play on. If so have you ever noticed that the table you use is fairly high. From the table to the floor is about 1 metre.

Another fact is that an adult bellybutton is about 1 metre from the ground.

To be specific a metre is 10 dm, 100 cm and 1000 mm.

I hope this letter has given you the information you needed about the metre in the advanced world of **MATH**.

This grade 4 student demonstrates the ability to think and write accurately about a math concept by relating it to everyday life.

What goes in a kindergarten portfolio?

Items in a kindergarten portfolio – Children entering school for the first time are at various stages of learning. The teacher will plan the content of the kindergarten portfolio based on curriculum outcomes and the developmental stages of learning. To show growth over time, when students are unable to read and write, takes innovative thought as well as careful planning. At regular intervals, the teacher and students should reflect as a group on what they have learned, on their successes, and on how they can improve. These discussions will provide the vocabulary needed and help prepare the students for self-assessment. Reflections by the students on what they have learned would occur informally and orally, with the teacher, possibly, scribing what they say.

November 28. Excitement is contagious!!! We went to the kindergarten classrooms after school today and were so impressed by what we saw. They have devised a way for even the youngest students to be involved in portfolios. They explained how they created a mock portfolio, using a teddy bear named Percival as the owner of the portfolio. They demonstrated the developmental stages of learning through Percival's portfolio. It's the model they will use when implementing the student portfolios in their classrooms. They have created an ingenious assessment tool for students who are just beginning to read and write. What a great way to introduce the concept to both students and parents!

Kay and Shirley-Dale

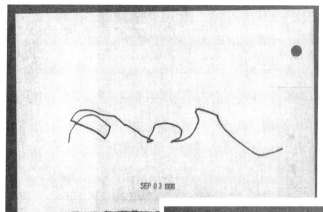

SEP 0 3 1996

JAN 0 7 1996

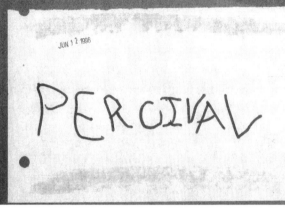

JUN 1 2 1996

SEP -2

A kindergarten portfolio might include printing samples and drawings that show progress over the term or full year.

February 12. Our staff has been immersed in district in-service workshops on writing this term. Time seems to be the enemy when we try to cover all the writing outcomes in language arts. However, after studying all the different genres of writing, I can see possible ways to include the outcomes. I can teach report writing in science, explanation in math class and even exposition in social studies. Now some of the pressure has been removed. The writing my grade 2 students produced in their science reports impresses me. These will be strong writing pieces for them to include in their portfolios. I would have thought teaching research skills to this age group was an impossibility in the days when we had science fairs and the parents did most of the research.

Kay

The Portfolio Program and Cross-Curricular Applications

How do you incorporate all genres of writing in the portfolio?

The advantage of language arts criteria overlapping with criteria in other subjects is quite apparent when the teacher looks for ways to include all the genres of writing in a portfolio. The genres of writing can be incorporated easily in other subjects. The elementary teacher, who generally teaches most subjects to one class, can even *plan* his or her curriculum and lessons so that the students produce specific pieces of work in different subjects as examples of writing in different genres. This reduces the pressure on the teacher to teach all the genres of writing during the time allotted for language arts. Some writing genres are naturally more appropriate for certain subjects. Report writing, for example, fits well and can be taught easily in science, math or social studies class.

Teaching the genres of reading and writing in the elementary school begins in kindergarten. It is beneficial for the staff to meet and decide at what grade level each will be introduced to ensure that all genres have been taught by the end of the elementary school years. As students progress along a continuum of learning in each genre, they will become progressively more competent in writing it. In order for students to have success in the writing of essays, for example, they need to know what good essays sound like and what they look like. In other words, they need to be able to identify the characteristics of good essay writing and know the language and format of that genre.

How can teachers develop the different genres of writing across the curriculum to obtain samples for the students' portfolios?

We have had a lot of success in implementing the different genres of writing across the curriculum. The table on page 59 identifies the main writing genres, their purpose, and the kinds of written product associated with them.

Writing Genre	Purpose of Writing	Examples of Products
Narrative	to entertain and engage the reader in an imaginative experience.	stories, fables, legends, plays, folklore, historical biographies, myths, science fiction, ballads, poetry
Recount	to retell or recount a past experience	newspaper accounts, letters, reading response, journals, learning logs, retellings, biographies, autobiographies
Report	to present information clearly in factual texts	newspaper reports, subject-specific reports
Procedure	to list a sequence of events or steps to show the way to do something	instruction manuals, recipes, science experiments, math procedures
Explanation	to explain how things come to be the way they are or how things work	handbooks, explanations of how and why
Exposition	to critically evaluate ideas, to persuade using logical reasoning and point of views	essays, letters, policies, critical reviews, advertisements

Adapted from First Steps Writing Resource Book

Quick Tip

Many points on the general writing criteria chart are applicable to all genres of writing, but each genre has its own specific language features and forms.

How do you teach report writing and integrate it in subjects other than language arts?

The following steps for teaching report writing and research skills can be adapted for teaching any genre of non-fiction writing. Science class creates a particularly meaningful setting for teaching report writing in grade 2.

Steps for Teaching Report Writing
1. Reading, listening, discussing and examining • Identify curriculum outcomes and choose the topic. • Collect books for modeling, for shared reading and for independent reading. • Read information text and model how to begin research by examining the parts of the book. For example, the Table of Contents is important for targeting the area you are researching. • Make comparisons during shared reading to show students how information text differs from narrative text. For example, in an information text it is not necessary to begin reading from the start of the book. • Have students read independently or in pairs and discuss how to research. Examine a number of books on the chosen topic so that students gain insight into the characteristics of a report.

Steps for Teaching Report Writing

2. Writing

- Provide an exemplar of a good report. It should meet all the criteria for the report project students will work on.
- Focus on a specific part of the chosen topic. Use the exemplar as a model while reading through it with the students. Refer to the model in a discussion of how to research.
- Have students share their prior knowledge on the chosen topic. The teacher records information on chart paper or on the chalkboard. Refer to an information text resource if there is a question of correctness related to the content.
- Write questions that identify what the students need or want to know about the chosen topic.
- On chart paper or the chalkboard, with class input, prepare a web or outline of what the students need or want to know.
- Using the web or outline, engage in shared writing of the report with the class.
- Give students an opportunity to look at books and choose their topic to research.
- In the allotted class and homework time, students should research their topic, and then follow the writing process to prepare their project.
- When students have written what they learned, celebrate the completion of the project by displaying their writing and a photograph of the project on the bulletin board.

3. Parent Involvement in Teaching Report Writing

- Send home a note informing parents of the project and the criteria for competent report writing.
- Emphasize that the parent may guide the student in the research, but the project is the student's responsibility. Parents may help the student search for books, magazines and other artifacts in their home and public libraries on the chosen topic and the student may bring these items to school. Explain that much of the research and writing of the project will be completed in school.
- Invite parents to the class exhibition and presentation of projects.

4. Portfolio Connections

- Guide students in constructing the report writing criteria chart.
- Display the criteria chart for the class to use when they revise their reports, assess their own work and write their goals.
- Students will choose their best piece from various works done during the project for their portfolio.

March 15. I wanted to teach expository writing and decided that it would be best if the students in my grade six class could write about real issues so I devised a procedure for Friday mornings. It was a success story and these classes became the most exciting experiences of the week, the discussion and debate sometimes carrying over for days and even weeks. They wrote and talked about guns and war, election issues, world hunger, fighting in sports, earthquakes, animal rights and many, many other issues. My position was to allow for freedom of speech but to supply additional facts or the history behind them. This was the most effective way to teach the rubrics for expository writing and I am in awe of the depth of understanding and the critical analysis that is possible with students at this age.

Shirley-Dale

What procedure works best for including expository writing in a portfolio?

Expository writing is a natural genre to use in social studies. One of the easiest ways to teach students the criteria for good expository writing is with the use of newspapers.

Criteria Chart and Procedures for Teaching Expository Writing

Procedures	Criteria
• Gather day-old newspapers and place them on a table in the classroom. • Invite the students to select a paper and browse. • Have the students choose an article that interests them and highlight key words, mainly in the first paragraph. • Ask the students to cut out the article and glue it into a notebook. • Have the students write one paragraph to summarize the content/issue in the article. • Ask the students to write their own critical thoughts about the article. • Refer the students to the expository writing criteria chart. • Have the students share the major issue through discussion and debate. • The teacher clarifies points and leads the discussion.	• Write in order to talk someone into something. • Believe in the topic you are writing about. • Use the thesaurus and dictionary. • Back up your ideas with good reasons. • Use phrases such as "It is believed that…" and "Concern is shown about…" • Stick to the point. • The beginning paragraph tells the writer's point of view. • Each paragraph tells a different point. • Use different kinds of action words. • Research to make sure the points are correct. • Write the last paragraph to sum up the main points. • Have correct punctuation.

This chart provides the full procedure for teaching expository writing with the use of newspapers. Adjacent to the procedure is a sample of a class-made criteria chart for expository writing.

Are there standardized criteria for math writing?

There has been a shift in the approach to teaching mathematics, from a procedural approach to a conceptual one in which reasoning and making real-world connections are central to the objectives. Math writing is one of the best ways for students to communicate their understandings and to make meaningful connections. The act of writing forces a slow-down in the thought process and leads to a deeper examination of a problem, making it readily apparent to teachers and to students what the students know and don't know.

However, a problem arises when students try to evaluate their own math writing using a general writing criteria chart. It is intrinsically more difficult for students to put their math thinking into words. When students use the points on a general writing criteria chart to help them choose their best math pieces, the criteria do not *quite* fit. A writing sample that would pass as competent in language arts, could still clearly demonstrate that the student did not understand the math concept.

How We Helped Our Students Develop Math Writing Skills

Our experience with math writing began when the provincial standardized test results were reported, and we were concerned because our school had tested exceptionally low in mathematics. As a staff, we had to look closely at the way we were teaching math and to devise a plan to remedy the situation. The staff began to focus more on math in professional readings and in discussions. As two teachers on that staff, we began to think about math writing. Perhaps it could be used to target the conceptual approach to math that was lacking. We asked ourselves, "Why do we want children to write in math? How can we motivate them to write? Will math writing help produce better math students?" We began to focus more on writing in our math classes.

We then decided to include math writing in the portfolio program. We had experienced success in having students select their best pieces from their reading and writing curriculum, but with the inclusion of math writing, we hit some major roadblocks.

We began to look for articles relating to criteria for math writing to guide us in constructing class-made math writing criteria charts. We found that researchers were talking about the need for such a tool, but we could not find one. We met with a series of math educators at all levels, and we discovered that, at that time, one did not exist. We continued our research, reading everything we could find about math writing.

Still, nothing really suited our particular needs, so we developed a multi-aged project involving our grade 2 and grade 6 classes. This project was math research whereby we documented the math writings of our students over an extended period of time. Our own observations were in the form of a shared journal. Our research gave us an in-depth look at math writing, and it resulted in our developing a mathematics assessment tool in the form of a math writing criteria chart.

How is a math writing criteria chart developed?

The general procedure for developing a math writing criteria chart is essentially the same as developing any criteria chart. However, developing criteria for math writing is a bit more complicated.

To construct a good math writing criteria chart, teachers and students need to use "math talk" to clarify and share ideas. Math talk provides the language for students and the teacher to use in the construction of the math writing criteria chart.

Language plays an important role in math learning in all grades. The foundation for math writing is set in kindergarten. When students talk to adults in the class or to other students, talking helps them make sense of what they are doing. Whether students are engaged in one-to-one matching, building with blocks, constructing a 3-D model or problem solving, they should be verbalizing their thoughts and observations. This gives the teacher an opportunity to discover if the student has any misconceptions and serves to inform instruction.

It is important in all subjects for the teacher to model the criteria and provide exemplars for the students. It is essential to do so for math writing as well.

Rubrics and criteria for mathematics might be available from the regional department of education or the local school board. However, if there are no standardized math-writing rubrics and criteria, the teacher and students must work together to design a math rubric, viewing examples of good, adequate and poor work. When they proceed to the next step, developing the criteria charts, they should focus on the specifics of math writing, including when to use diagrams, and how to present an example. Specific points such as these should be recorded on the chart. The more precise and clear the points about math writing, the easier it will be for students to assess their own work against the criteria chart.

The specifics of math writing can vary from grade to grade depending on the concepts and skills already learned or in the process of being developed. For example, a grade 2 math writing criteria chart might not be as detailed as a grade 6 math writing criteria chart. Grade 6 students have more experience and knowledge in both writing and mathematics than grade 2 students.

What Good Math Writers Do — Grade 2

1. Use drawings or diagrams.
2. Use math language.
3. Show you understand by giving examples.
4. Make sure the work is correct.
5. Use capitals and correct punctuation marks.
6. Make sure the work makes sense.

What Good Math Writers Do — Grade 6

1. Describe it as if the reader doesn't know math.
2. Give examples.
3. Make sure you are correct.
4. Make it readable (clear).
5. Use diagrams, graphs and pictures.
6. Use math words.
7. Try to tell it in more than one way.
8. Relate it to real life.
9. Get to the point.

These criteria charts for grades 2 and 6 show how the specifics of math writing can be similar but different in different grades.

November 4

I chose this piece because I used math words. I tell it in more than one way. I totally understand the concept and it is readable. I give examples and I get to the point.

My goal is to try and explain fractions in words so that if someone doesn't know math it helps them.

The grade 6 student who wrote this reflection to accompany a work sample clearly understood how to use math language to explain why the sample was his or her "best work."

November 1. I am amazed at how quickly many of the primary students pick up math terminology. They are fascinated with big words, and, after all my years of teaching, I am still surprised when they use various terms in the right context. It proves to me how important it is to expose students to the correct terminology. When I was reading their learning logs at home last night, my husband was impressed with the correct use of terms such as digit, angle, symmetrical, estimate and product.

Kay

The teacher can encourage the students to use math talk by asking "math talk questions" that will help students to develop the appropriate vocabulary for talking and writing in mathematics.

Math Talk Questions

- *Tell* me about the _____ (number 400, prime number, shape, fraction, coin) you like the most and why.
- *Tell* me how two _____ (shapes, numbers, patterns) are the same and how they are different.
- *Tell* me when you would use math at home, playing outside, in the mall, on a trip.
- That is an interesting answer. *Tell me more.*
- *I wonder what* _____ (would happen if there were no pennies).
- *I wonder if* _____ (our classroom is longer than 25 meters).
- Is there anything that *puzzled* you about _____ (addition, subtraction, multiplication, division, fractions…)
- Pretend you are a _____ (prime number, composite number, hexagon, quarter, decimal) and *tell about* yourself.
- *Explain* why _____ (multiplication is repeated addition).
- Can you *explain* (compare and discuss) it in another way?
- *Describe how* _____ (you use measurement in your daily life).
- How do you *know* that _____ $(345 + 256 - 444 = 157)$?
- **Who/what** am I? (use riddles)
- Does that *make sense?*
- *Does this remind you of another problem? Which one?*

How important is "talk" in any aspect of learning?

It is important that students in all grades and subjects be given opportunities to talk about what they are doing. Sharing ideas with partners, in small groups and in whole-class discussions helps students learn from each other. It helps them discover that there is more than one way to look at any problem and more than one way to solve it. Students need to use and understand the language of a genre or subject before they can use it effectively and correctly in writing. The teacher must be skilful in leading the talk and then be able to listen and gain insights from the students. This enables the teacher to guide them at the appropriate time and at the appropriate developmental level when the class is constructing the criteria chart.

How can all genres of writing be included in portfolios when the middle school teacher teaches only one or two subjects?

Ideally, by the time students begin middle school, they should at least have been introduced to the main genres of literature. The students may not have mastered the genres, but the basic genres should be familiar to them. The middle school teachers will then have the task of reviewing and extending the students' knowledge and understanding of the genres.

It makes sense that the challenge of teaching writing in all forms be shared by all teachers in all subjects. Teamwork is such an important part of the teaching process. Literacy across the curriculum has been advocated for years in the teaching arena. A team of teachers must know the curriculum outcomes thoroughly and share the teaching of them. With careful planning, a team of teachers can share the responsibility of teaching each writing genre to ensure that students progress naturally on a continuum of learning.

If a portfolio program is implemented through a team approach, students will have selected a variety of writing genres simply by choosing samples from each subject. If a teacher is working independently without the support of a team, on a portfolio program, the genres of writing most suitable for his or her teaching subjects can be included.

June 9. I am ready to write the final report cards of the year. I have lots of data collected from tests, anecdotal notes from observations, running records, writing samples and the portfolios. When I think about these assessment tools, I am reminded of a question that was asked at our last Portfolio Workshop. "Do you mark the portfolios?" What a difficult question that is. For primary students, giving the portfolio a mark doesn't seem to serve any purpose. I don't need to put a mark on the whole portfolio to know their achievements. Yet the samples the students selected will definitely influence their final mark since they are representative of what they know and can do. I feel strongly that the end product is important but the process my students went through is so very important. They have learned so much about themselves as learners. From viewing the portfolios, even my struggling students have made progress. They may not have reached all the outcomes required for a grade two student, but they have certainly grown in all areas and feel good about themselves as learners. I may see the value of putting a mark on portfolios for older students but at this level it would take some strong convincing.

Kay

Portfolio assessment can be used in any subject. The rationale and procedure for constructing a subject-specific portfolio is the same as those for constructing a comprehensive portfolio. The subject teacher will have spent time researching and aligning curriculum outcomes and instructional techniques and tools with the appropriate assessment strategies. The subject teacher uses subject-specific criteria charts and scoring rubrics. The points on the criteria charts will vary according to the learning outcomes of that particular subject.

The following model may serve as a starting point for planning the contents of a portfolio in any subject area.

Once the students have selected their pieces of work for the portfolio, do you mark or grade the portfolio?

There is no simple answer to this question. There has been an on-going debate about this issue among educators for years. Portfolio assessment threads itself throughout the teaching and learning process all year. The skills gained in making and using criteria, organizing, self-assessing and goal setting are life skills. When students are involved in this process, they are encouraged to become metacognitive regarding their learning. The portfolio provides the concrete evidence that they use to judge their own progress and achievements. They collaborate with the teacher and learn that their judgment is valued.

If the teacher marks the cumulative portfolio, there is a possibility that all the positive attributes of the portfolio process could be undermined. Students may put more effort and energy into getting a higher mark, or even to pass, than into articulating their own strengths and needs. Once more, they may begin to rely on the judgment of the teacher, foregoing all that they have learned about

Suggested Content for Subject-Specific Portfolios

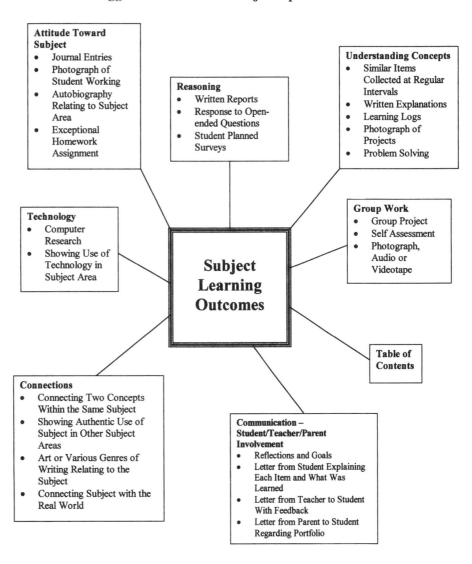

self-assessment. Their credibility will have been weakened. The realistic reflections and goals they have set for themselves will have been replaced with those set by the teacher or an external evaluator. In short, the teacher will be again taking on the role of sole evaluator.

Whether the whole portfolio is marked or not marked, however, the process and the product influence the teacher. Portfolio assessment is such an integral part of the teaching and learning process that it is does influence the final mark, either formally or informally.

The teacher and student have been working together throughout the year assessing the same selections. Using class-made performance criteria, the developmental level of each selection should be no surprise to either the student or the teacher at the end of the school year.

If a teacher, a school, a district or a nation decides that a formal mark is to be given on student portfolios, there are some points to be considered:

- The ideal situation is for students to be involved in a portfolio program throughout their elementary school years, starting in kindergarten. This is the introductory phase. In the early years, the students are getting to know themselves as learners and are beginning to make decisions about their work as part of the assessment process. When these same students reach middle and high school, they should recognize the elements of a good portfolio and be more prepared to understand the rudiments of a portfolio marking system.
- Older students may put more effort into the portfolio if they know they are going to be awarded a final mark.
- If the portfolios are to be marked, teachers should work together to build a reliable scoring system. A class-made rubric can be a powerful tool for students when they construct and evaluate their portfolios. It is essential that students, teachers and parents understand the rubric for what constitutes a high quality portfolio. The students must have a clear vision of the end product and what it takes to get there.

June 12. This is grade 6 report-card time, and I have collected the materials I will use to make the final evaluation, portfolios being among them. As my students were selecting their final samples this year, one of them asked, "Will you be marking our portfolios?" When I said, "No" they were disappointed. It's interesting that I have never mentioned marks in relation to the portfolios, but there it is again. The whole world wants marks. I could actually develop a rubric and mark them, but something is telling me not to. It would be like breaking trust to tell some of them that, after all their work, they still aren't making the grade. Yet, they do have to know, in the grand scheme of things, where they stand. It really is a conundrum. If I marked their portfolios, would they be as rich in self-evaluation and creativity or would the portfolios all look the same? If the students center on the mark, I would again be sole evaluator. On the other hand, in the upper grades, do they mean anything to them without a mark?

Shirley-Dale

5

Sharing the Portfolio: Conferencing

> We seldom see growth on a daily basis. It's only when we look at blocks of time do we suddenly recognize change. The portfolios are a fabulous work in progress. Bravo!
>
> – Parent of grade 6 student

November 30. It's a relief that parent-teacher interviews are over for this term. We're all over-tired, and the general feeling is that we were rushed off our feet. Even the mention of parent-teacher interviews conjures up a picture of long lines of parents in chairs outside the classroom door waiting for their turn to see us. Even with careful scheduling, time is never on our side. In the staff room this morning, we were talking about this, and the subject of portfolios came up. A couple of us used pieces from the portfolios to back up the report card marks, but, really, we didn't do them justice. The students who worked so hard on their portfolios weren't there to show them off. Some of the students were even waiting outside the classroom door, fretting, and wondering what was being said.
Shirley-Dale and I have been reading and talking to teachers in our workshops about student-led conferences. Maybe the time is right for our staff to, at least, begin to look at new ways to make these interviews more productive.

Kay

Sharing the Portfolio

To improve their learning, students need to receive appropriate and focused feedback, from both teachers and parents; they also need to know how to assess their own learning. The preparation of a portfolio in itself is a powerful learning tool. However, sharing the contents of the portfolio is also a significant part of a portfolio program.

Portfolio programs offer a unique and authentic way for parents to see exactly what the student — their child — is doing in class. A portfolio gives parents hard evidence of their child's abilities and provides insight into the report card marks their child receives. In addition, a portfolio is a way for students to develop self-confidence and to take pride in their achievements.

The question now becomes, "How do you present a child's portfolio to his or her parent(s)?" In this chapter, we look at parent-teacher interviews, and the advantages of presenting portfolios to parents in a conference with or without the teacher present.

Meetings, Interviews and Conferences

What are "parent-teacher meetings?"

Parent-teacher meetings are times when the parent(s) of a child meets with the child's teacher(s) to review the progress of the child. In the past, these meetings were called "parent-teacher interviews." The word "interview" implies a meeting between two people, where one obtains information from the other. In recent years, the word "conference" has replaced the word "interview." The word "conference" connotes "a group of people sharing information." This change in terminology represents a major shift in the way educators think about communicating with parents.

With students taking more ownership of their own learning and assessment, it is a natural progression to move toward a conference format. There is some flexibility in how the conference can be conducted. Each approach differs in structure and each serves its own purpose when informing parents of the progress of their children.

What is the traditional approach to parent-teacher meetings?

The traditional approach, the "parent-teacher interview," has been in practice for many years. The parent-teacher interview is a formal, scheduled meeting where the teacher informs the parents of the student's progress. The student, the major stakeholder in the process, is not present. Information about the student's performance level is strictly between the teacher and parent(s), with the student being a secondhand recipient. There are times during the school year when a traditional parent-teacher interview is beneficial. The parent and the teacher may want to discuss confidential matters without the student present.

What are "student-led conferences?"

"Student-led conferences" are meetings attended by the student, teacher and parent(s). There are a number of different formats for a student-led conference. In each case, the student is an active participant.

Student-led conferences are an excellent way for the student to share his or her portfolio with the parent(s). These conferences provide a time for the student to present his or her portfolio to his or her parent(s). Conferences also provide an opportunity for the student, parent(s) and teacher to discuss the work in the portfolio and the reasons for the student's level of achievement.

Are portfolios required for student-led conferences?

One of the most important parts of the portfolio process is the chance to share the portfolio at the conference. Because the students have constructed the portfolios and selected the sample pieces of work themselves, it holds real meaning for them. Ownership is a key aspect of portfolio programs and portfolio assessment. The portfolio process is not something *done to* students, it is a process *done by* students.

In order for students to conduct successful conferences, they need to have a selection of work to show as concrete evidence of their performance. A portfolio is more effective than a "work file" for various reasons. A portfolio is less cumbersome, it is organized and it is representative of the full term's work. The student-chosen samples of "best work" in a portfolio are the basis of the discussion at the conference. During the conference with their parents, the students are to talk about their work confidently, compare it to their previous work, discuss their own development and growth over time, and review the goals they have set.

The teacher orchestrates the steps in planning the student-led conference, but, often, the success of the conference depends on how well the students are prepared. It is the teacher's job to ensure that the students know what to do and why they are involved in the process.

Parents, Portfolio Programs and Conferencing

How do you educate parents about a portfolio program and student-led conferences?

Educating the parents about a portfolio program and student-led conferences is extremely important. They are probably not familiar with this program and method of assessment. It could differ from what they experienced as students. Therefore, they are often apprehensive and have many questions about the validity of such a practice. They may not understand why and how the changes can be of benefit. The teacher needs to begin educating the parents about these changes well before the student-led conferences are going to be held. These are some ideas to consider:

Hold information sessions – Early in the school year, consider sending a letter home to parents, advising them that the school will be implementing a portfolio program. Perhaps at the "Meet the Teacher Night," the principal could lead an information session to inform all the parents that portfolios and portfolio assessment are components of the school's balanced learning program. The philosophy and the long- and short-term benefits of portfolios must be clearly communicated at this time. Parents should be encouraged to ask questions. The school must assure that all stakeholders understand the goals, outcomes and expectations of a portfolio program and portfolio assessment.

In the classroom session of "Meet the Teacher Night," the teacher can tell the parents about the specific details of a portfolio program and how portfolios will be used in student-led conferences. Parents should be informed of the expectations for their child at the grade level in all subjects. Portfolios from previous years, if available, would be beneficial for parents to view.

Send out newsletters – Weekly or monthly, various articles addressing educational issues might be sent home with students in a duo-tang or other form of parent information booklet. A number of these articles could focus on portfolio programs and portfolio assessment. For example, articles on student-led conferences would be included before the scheduled conferences. Articles that are sent home to parents should be easy to read and understood, and they should be free from teacher jargon and confusing terminology. It can be useful to leave a space after an article, so that parents' can send back their responses and questions. This approach to educating the parents allows them to read and reflect in the privacy of their own homes. The feedback from parents should give the teachers insight into the parents' understanding, which will lead to better education for all.

Sample Letter to Parents

Date_____

School _____

Teacher and/or Principal _____

Dear Parents,

During this first term, your child will be involved in many exciting learning experiences. One of these will be the construction of a portfolio. Our school is pleased to announce that all students in the school will keep a portfolio this year. The portfolio is just **one** of a variety of assessment methods that will be used throughout the year.

A portfolio program allows your child to take an active part in his or her assessment process. During the month of September, the teacher is collecting the first piece of work your child completes in each subject. These samples will be placed in what is called your child's "working portfolio." After these initial samples are collected, your child will choose all future pieces of work that go into his or her portfolio during the year. By participating in this process, your child will learn to make decisions, self-evaluate, and set goals.

You will be updated on the progress of the portfolios throughout the year.

Some parents may be familiar with this method of assessment if their child has been involved with a portfolio program before. For parents who are not familiar with portfolios, we encourage you to come and see what a portfolio looks like at the "Meet the Teacher Night," when portfolios will be explained and discussed in greater detail.

We look forward to meeting you on _____(Meet the Teacher Night date). If you have any questions that you would like addressed before the above date, please feel free to write them in the space provided below.

Questions

_____

_____

_____

_____

_____

Send work home with the students – Early in the school year, the teacher should identify the developmental level of each student, and then inform the parent(s). At regular intervals, parents should see evidence of their child's work, accompanied by comments regarding his or her progress. This practice is particularly important for students who are not meeting grade-level expectations. There should be no surprises for parents when the report card is sent home.

It is also helpful to invite the students' parents to visit the classroom a number of times throughout the year, other than reporting time. Individual teachers or the school might want to consider providing training sessions for interested parents, enabling them to work in the classroom as trained volunteers.

April 14. At our workshop today, we got some negative comments from a teacher speaking from a parent's perspective. She was adamant that student-led conferences were a waste of time! She had visited her son's school and he presented his portfolio. She was unimpressed because she and her husband had already seen all of the contents, signed them and sent them back to the school. This was obviously a case of the son's teachers paying "lip service" to the idea of student-led conferencing and not understanding the importance of the students' role in selecting the portfolio pieces, reflecting on them and setting goals for the next term. The portfolio really is useless if it is just a collection of tests and assignments.

Kay

Should parents see items before they go into the portfolios?

The portfolio is not just a collection of work. It is an assessment tool kept by the students and it represents what they deem to be their best work. Parents may or may not have seen the samples prior to the student-led conferences. Assignments, projects and tests may have been sent home for parents to examine, and some teachers require that these be signed by parents and returned to school. Although these items may be contained in the portfolio as teacher-chosen pieces, the students focus on selecting items from their work files, notebooks, or writing folders.

Reflecting on their own growth and articulating it in the student-led conference is no small feat for students. They are accountable for their own work and often put forth more effort if they know they have an audience. It is their responsibility to explain to their parents why they received a certain mark. It is no longer solely the teacher who is telling the parents what the students have achieved and where they need improvement. The students make a commitment to their parents, their teacher and themselves on how they are going to reach their goals. The parents become aware of what areas need improvement and can give support towards accomplishing the goals.

In the past, many parents were simply asked to sign tests and return them to the school. There was little discussion of why the student received a mark or where improvement was needed. Student-led conferencing may be the first time that some families have met to discuss the specifics of their children's work. The student has an opportunity to share his or her work, and realize that his or her parent(s) is interested and supportive. The parent recognizes the effort put forth by the child.

How do parents react to student-led conferences?

Many parents are surprised that students have learned to manage, organize and make decisions about their own work. Often, the experience gives parents a new respect for their children when they observe them as leaders. Some parents comment that they did not realize their children had learned as much as they demonstrated at the conference. As the students explain where they need improvement, both the parent and the teacher see concepts that are unclear to the student. Parents, students and teachers have an opportunity to discuss goals and how they are going to be reached.

Portfolio Questionnaire

Child's Name   Date Mar 24/

We value your feedback on the effectiveness of this portfolio. Please complete questionnaire below:

1. Does this portfolio help you have a better understanding of your child's development? Please explain.

I can see from one year to the next that there is ~~different~~ definate improvement in his work. It's good to have the samples from previous years to compare

2. Please add any comments or suggestions about the use of portfolios as a measure of your child's growth.

I would like to see some of his tests kept and put in the portfolio I must admit, I'm of the age where we were given grades by the percentage marks, and so tests that show he made 80% or 50% for example tell me how things are going.

Parent feedback about student-led conferences

72

Parents' Comments About Portfolio Presentations

Parents Speak Out About Portfolio Presentations

"We turned our living room over to our daughter for her presentation. We couldn't believe how well prepared and organized she was. Her interview took about 45 minutes and was very informative and interesting. We think these portfolios are a great idea and a good confidence booster too!" (Parent of student showing portfolio at home)

"Even though it may seem like a small task, it was fun to see our son use some organizational and presentational skills. He was excited to show us his work." (Grade 4)

"The portfolio supplements the report card only by showing a student's progression. It does not help if parents do not know where the benchmarks are for the stages of progression. A child may show little improvement and still meet the standards on the report card. Or a child could show considerable improvement in the portfolio and not come close to meeting the standards on the report card." (Grade 3)

"I think portfolios are a great way of getting the children to analyze their own work and feel proud of their improvements that they can see by comparing. Having children set goals for themselves and checking to see how many goals they have stuck to gives the child a sense of self-satisfaction." (Grade 5)

"It would be nice to see my daughter keep the same portfolio from year to year, adding things to see how she improves." (Grade 2)

"This is the first time my daughter has offered to share her work with me." (Grade 8)

"I believe this is an excellent tool to show a child's strengths and weaknesses and it gives the child an opportunity to be critical about his own work." (Grade 7)

"I watched my son present his portfolio and I was quite impressed but I still don't know where he stands in the class. I want to make an appointment to have an interview with just the teacher to find out how he is really making out." (Grade 6)

"It was a lot of fun to visit the classroom and see our daughter working and talking about the various learning centers. I was surprised at how much she is really learning in activities that look like play to me." (Kindergarten)

What do you do if students are prepared for a conference and the parents will not attend?

There are various reasons why some parents do not want to come to the school to attend conferences with a teacher. In many cases, these are parents who had negative experiences at school themselves and they feel intimidated. They view the teacher as an authority figure and they do not want to relive the past. When they know that their own child is in charge of the interview, they are often more willing to attend. The focus is on their child, not on them. These parents' views and attitudes gradually change as they learn to see themselves as contributors and an important part of the whole process.

If parents will still not attend conferences, regardless of the format, there are other ways to approach the problem. All the students in the class will follow the same preparation procedure for showing the portfolio at a conference. The teacher will make every effort to encourage parent-attendance, making individual contact, finding times that are more convenient for the parent(s), and generally building a rapport. If parents still choose not to attend, a home conference might be arranged for the student and the parents. A written response can be returned to the school after the home conference takes place.

Planning and Scheduling Student-Led Conferences

March 30. We are still talking in the staff room about our experiences with student-led conferences. It is like a game we played and won. We can't let it drop. The question arose as to whether the students took the conferences as seriously as we did. One staff member told us that the twin boys in her grade 1 class came to the conference in three-piece suits, their hair slicked back, their portfolios under their arms like briefcases. One waited outside quietly while his brother showed his portfolio to his parents and then he took his turn. Regardless of what the conferences meant to others, it was certainly serious business for them.

Kay

March 30. I think that the question of the importance of the conferences, which we have just completed, is answered in the attire of my grade six students. Although I didn't once mention what they should wear, I noticed that they dressed in their best clothes. Most of the boys wore shirts instead of t-shirts and a couple of them actually wore ties. This might seem like a simple thing but, to me, it shows the importance that the parents as well as the students placed on the interviews.

Shirley-Dale

When do you conduct student-led conferences — after each reporting period?

This might vary depending on the school, the teaching team or an individual teacher. In some schools, the entire school implements student-led conferences. In other schools, it is the decision of a team or an individual teacher.

Ideally, the students would be capable of taking the lead in conferences at any time of the year, but, due to the many demands placed on the teacher's time during the first term of the school year, a first-term student-led conference is not always possible. It often works better to have the first formal interview with only the parent(s) present, as the teachers and parent(s) may need to exchange and discuss confidential information.

The second reporting period is an ideal time for students to be in charge and lead the conference. This allows students enough time to become familiar with the process and to feel confident in taking the lead in conducting the conference. After the final reporting period, a conference would occur only upon the request of the parents or the teacher.

What things should the teacher consider when setting up a schedule for conferencing?

The key to student-led conferencing is flexibility and creativity when setting up the appointments. Allow at least twenty minutes for each conference. This takes thought, brainstorming by the staff or team and careful planning. Think through the class list and the parents involved.

The following questions can provide some guidance.

- Is it absolutely necessary that certain, specific parents attend?
- Have any parents requested a traditional interview for various reasons?
- Are there some parents who have been in constant contact with the teacher and who have visited the classroom many times during the term? Could these parents have the option of viewing the portfolio at home?
- Which students might be capable of taking the portfolio home and conducting a student-led conference successfully on their own?
- Which students would benefit from three-way conferences?
- Are any students ready for student-led conferences with the teacher as facilitator for three or four groups at once?
- Can conferences be scheduled other than the traditional afternoon/evening?

Mixed-Approach Conferences

<table>
<tr>
<td colspan="3">Traditional
(Parents/Teacher)

Jack — parents requested

Joel — parents requested

Anne — parents work at night

James — parents requested</td>
<td colspan="3">Two-Way Conference
(Parents/Student/Teacher Roving)</td>
</tr>
<tr>
<td colspan="3"></td>
<td>Group 1
Julie
Andrew
Maria
Michael</td>
<td>Group 2
John
Suzanne
Tom
Betty</td>
<td>Group 3
Robert
Joy
Lisa
Dan</td>
</tr>
<tr>
<td colspan="3"></td>
<td colspan="3">(Above average students)</td>
</tr>
<tr>
<td colspan="3">Three-Way Conferences
(Parents/Student/Teacher)

Jillian — excellent, being videoed

Glen — shy

Harry — hearing impaired

Kelly — transfer student, 1st attempt</td>
<td colspan="3">Showing Portfolio at Home
(Student/Parents)
(during the week)

Amanda — parent works in classroom
Brittni
Alicia
Todd
Greg
Jordan — parent works in classroom
(strong students)</td>
</tr>
<tr>
<td colspan="3">Four-Five Way Conferences
(Student Support Services, Resource Teacher, Parents, Principal, Student, Teacher)

George — IEP

Jason — Behavioral adjustments

Kathleen — Gifted</td>
<td colspan="3">Schedule
Monday   4 p.m. – 6:30 p.m.   traditional
Tuesday   4 p.m. – 5:30 p.m.   4–5 way
Wednesday — Parent/Teacher scheduled night
3:00 p.m. Jillian   6:30 p.m.   Group 1
3:30 p.m. Glen   7:15 p.m.   Group 2
4:00 p.m. Kelly   8:00 p.m.   Group 3
4:30 p.m. Justin
5:00 p.m. Harry
Thursday – Return Portfolios
Friday — Tidy up and celebrate.</td>
</tr>
</table>

Use a round table for conferences. It suggests equality for all participants.

February 1. It all looks ideal on paper. We've been studying this literature on student-led conferences all winter and one big question looms large: How do we find the time? We will go ahead with it anyway, each of us left on our own to work out the details. This is the plan. We will each do what we feel we can handle and report on our successes and challenges directly following the interviews. It will be interesting to see how all of this works out.

Shirley-Dale

Preparing for Student-Led Conferences

A Few Days Before the Conference

- Understand the purposes and benefits of student-led conferences.
- Create an atmosphere of excitement for the upcoming event.
- Guide students in using criteria-charts to select and reflect on their work and to set goals.
- Model the presentation of a portfolio for the students.
- Schedule time for students to role-play and practice presenting their portfolios.
- Put the portfolios in a location that is easy to access at the conference.
- Help the class design and write invitations, requesting the presence of the parents on a specific day at a convenient time.
- Copy the Student-Led Conference Checklist.

The Day of the Conference

- Collect the following materials to be placed on the round table for the student-led conference:
  - student-led conference checklist
  - baselines samples or work samples from the previous term accompanied by reflections and goals in a specific colored folder
  - present-term selections accompanied by reflections and goals in a different colored folder
  - paper and pencil for note-taking during conference
  - tape recorder, hard copy of reading selections and audiotapes of reading selections from two reporting periods (optional; at teacher's discretion)
  - sheet for parents' post-conference reflection and comments
  - guest book for parents to sign
- Review the steps on the Student-Led Conference Checklist with the class.
- Set up the conference table at the end of the day.

The Day After the Conference

- Contribute to class discussion stating the successes and improvements needed for future conferences.
- Share positive feedback and suggestions from parents, other teachers and the principal.
- Celebrate!

Student-Led Conference Checklist

Conducting the Conference

___✓___ *Check off each step as you complete it.*

___1. Make an appointment with your parent(s).

___2. Arrive with your parent(s).

___3. Have your parent(s) sign the guest book if one is used.

___4. Take out your first-term samples.

___5. Show both samples together. Explain how you have improved and what you have learned. Tell your parent(s) your new goals.

Check off each subject when you finish presenting your work from that subject

___✓___ Math

_____ Science

_____ Social studies

_____ Language arts

_____ Health

_____ Technology

_____ French

_____ Others

___6. Show your artwork and response.

___7. Ask your parent(s) to fill in the portfolio questionnaire and place it in your portfolio.

___8. Thank your parent(s).

Implementing Student-Led Conferences

Quick Tip

Prepare thoroughly for student-led conferences. Prepare the students, prepare the parents and be prepared as a teacher.

Does every teacher on a staff have to conduct student-led conferences at the same time?

When teachers are in the beginning stages of changing a long-established practice, such as conducting traditional parent-teacher interviews, it is wise for them to think through the process of change carefully. The teachers need to cogitate, to plan, and to find their own comfort zone. Change takes time, and each teacher should be allowed the freedom to proceed at his or her own pace.

Are there different ways to conduct student-led conferences?

Student-led conferences can be set up in different ways. In any student-led conference, except in cases where a student has shared his or her portfolio at home, the teacher should be available to provide additional information and support for both the students and the parents.

Teacher as Facilitator – The student leads the conference, viewing the portfolio with his or her parents. The student, to showcase the best work of the term, has constructed the portfolio. Present-term work samples are compared with the previous-term samples, improvement is noted, and goals are discussed. Often, more than one conference is taking place in the classroom at the same time. The teacher is facilitating, adding comments as needed and, generally, overseeing the whole procedure.

Three-Way Conference – The teacher, the parents and the student are all present at the conference. For the first part of the conference, the student leads, presenting the portfolio by showing the items selected for the best work of the term. He or she compares them with previous samples, explaining why the new samples were chosen. The student points out the areas of growth and discusses the goals for the next term. The teacher is there to support the student and to add comments where needed. During the second part of the conference, the teacher shows supporting evidence for the student's remarks and addresses his or her recorded observations in various subjects and situations. This is the time the teacher discusses the report card and shows the rubrics and criteria charts, as well as grade-level expectations. The student will add specifics to verify the teacher's observations. Parents are free to comment and question throughout the conference.

March 20. Student-led conferences are over, and, believe it or not, I feel energized by the whole experience. It was one intensive week! It felt a bit like a carnival, beginning with a big kick-off, a big hype and ending rather quietly, with some serious insights and reflections. When I do this again, I may change some facets of the process, but I will definitely keep the one-week idea. I think it helps keep the energy high. My students feel good about themselves as evaluators, and I feel good about them. We have come through new waters together, and it is as if we now have a pact or a bond. Today we put the portfolios away until late May or early June, when we will begin readying ourselves for the last reporting period of the year.

Shirley-Dale

Five Teachers' Experiences With Student-Led Conferences

The following scenarios describe the early attempts of five teachers in one school as they move toward student-led conferences. These teachers have documented the pros and cons of their experiences with possible solutions for any drawbacks.

Whole-Class Student-Led Conferences

The Set Up

The classroom was set up for multiple conferences to occur at the same time. At each desk, a student led his or her conference, viewing the portfolio with his or her parent(s), comparing previous samples and setting goals. The teacher was in the classroom, facilitating, adding comments if needed, and, generally, overseeing the whole procedure. If parents felt that the student-led conference did not provide adequate information, they were given the option of making an appointment for an interview with the teacher alone.

Advantages	Drawbacks	Possible Remedies
• having simultaneous multiple conferences was a good way to deal with the time factor • the students were in full control and the teacher, as the observer, was able to make valuable notes	• noise was a problem because of the number of people in the room at the same time • note taking was limited for each student	• have a maximum of four students presenting at one time

Kindergarten Student-Led Conferences

The Set Up

Parents were invited to accompany their children to the classroom. The teacher, to show the learning outcomes in the curriculum, had targeted four familiar learning centers and displayed the outcomes at the station. The students led their parents to each centre and engaged in the various activities. Parents were encouraged to ask their children what they had learned to do at each centre. At a signal, they rotated to the next activity. The teacher had made portfolios for the students and had them on display for the parents to view.

Advantages	Drawbacks	Possible Remedies
• most parents were highly impressed by what the students knew about their own learning and the actual learning outcomes in the activity-based centers • some were quite adept at verbalizing their own strengths; these students could have attempted to show their own portfolios to their parents	• some students needed constant coaching to be able to attend to the task	• scheduling would be more productive if the teacher were to select which students would participate in each one-hour slot • each group should be a mix of students at various developmental levels of learning so that the teacher will be more effective when facilitating • have a maximum of six students at a time to observe each hour

Individual Student-Led Conferences

The Set Up

The teacher set the schedule to begin one week before the regular parent-teacher interview day. Making use of the time slots before school began in the morning, noon hours and after school ensured that each student had at least a twenty-minute conference. The teacher, parents and student sat at the round table together, and the student presented the selections and reflections. The teacher observed and listened, giving comments only when intervention was necessary.

Advantages	Drawbacks	Possible Remedies
• students took the procedure very seriously and their performances and knowledge about their own strengths and goals were impressive • demonstrated that even young children can take responsibility for their own assessment	• time was still a problem	• select two or three students to interview at one time

Mixed Approach

The Set Up

The teacher scrutinized her class list carefully, placing the names into categories. It was urgent to see some parents at a conference, for various reasons, while some students were capable of showing their portfolios at home. A conference time was set up for the first group of parents and their children. The second group of parents was given the option of viewing the portfolio at home or making an appointment to view the portfolio with the teacher and the student at school. Ten students made an appointment with their parents and showed their portfolios at home. Those parents and students were to submit a written evaluation of the performance. Four parents requested traditional parent-teacher interviews, which were scheduled throughout the week. On parent-teacher night the remaining students presented their portfolios in the classroom, one student at a time, and the teacher added supporting comments and evidence during the second half of each conference.

Advantages	Drawbacks	Possible Remedies
• a valuable learning experience for the teacher • students were basically in control of the first half of the conference with the teacher there for support as they discussed their strengths and goals for the next term • even the struggling students had some knowledge of their progress with the portfolio samples to show as proof	• students who presented their portfolios at home did not have the added teacher support	• the teacher is the most knowledgeable about the student's learning, and there is really no substitute for the astute comments he or she could make regarding a student's progress

Four- and Five-Way Conferences

The Set Up

The classroom teacher, the parents and the student were joined by one or two other educators for the conferences. The resource teacher, the principal, the French teacher and the teacher's aid each played a role at one time or another in a number of classrooms. The students involved were those with Individual Education Plans, English Second Language programs, enrichment programs and behavioural problems. The student, to the best of his or her ability, presented the student portfolio with input from the other participants.

Advantages	Drawbacks	Possible Remedies
• students made an attempt to verbalize their own progress, even if only minimally • students were able to extend their observations with prompting from the educators present at the interview • demonstrated that even young children can take responsibility for their own assessment	• scheduling for the four or five-way conferences was somewhat complicated • prior to the conference, the teacher needed to spend extra time with the students to practice presenting their portfolio	• use this kind of conferencing in the second or final term, so that students need less practice time

At what grade level can teachers begin holding student-led conferences?

Student-led conferences can be held as early as kindergarten. It is a matter of readiness. The teacher must have a thorough knowledge and understanding of the pedagogy behind the concept. From there, it is a matter of taking the first steps toward implementation. This involves taking a risk, learning from the experience and making changes accordingly.

Is it feasible to try student-led conferences in middle school?

Student-led conferences are valuable information sessions in middle school for the same reasons they are important and valuable in elementary school.

The time factor is a particular concern in middle schools. A team approach seems to be the most viable method of accommodating hundreds of students in one reporting period. If each member of a teaching team sets up his or her homeroom for five student-led conferences, held every half hour, with four teachers on a team and four classrooms, twenty students could present their portfolios every half hour. To make it easier, the classrooms should be close to each other so the teachers, as facilitators, can rove from classroom to classroom. The students, presenting samples of work from all subjects, need to know that their teacher in each subject is available for assistance if they encounter difficulty.

If an individual teacher in middle school decides to embark upon student-led conferences, the scheduling requires a great deal of thought and resourcefulness. It may be necessary to schedule many students in one time period. When planning which students present their portfolios in each time slot, the students' independence, maturity and developmental levels are factors to consider.

March 19. All that I can say is "Wow!" I was so proud of my students today. I chose certain children to take part in three-way conferences and I could see the pride in their faces as they presented their work. I was pleasantly surprised at how well they could explain their reflections and identify where they needed improvement. It was their one-day to shine. In the past when they took tests home it wasn't always a time for celebration.

One parent had tears in her eyes as she watched her son. In the past, school was the place where she got bad reports from teachers but here she was seeing her son in a new light.

Kay

The Rewards of a Portfolio Program and Student-Led Conferences

Is student-led conferencing worth all the time and effort?

The skills involved in constructing a portfolio and presenting it at a student-led conference are life skills. When a student is given the opportunity to be involved in the critical and evaluative analysis that a portfolio requires, they will be ahead of the game. They come away equipped with skills that are necessary for future endeavors. The communication, decision-making and organizational skills will be invaluable for their career planning and in their personal lives.

The Rewards of Student-Led Conferences

Rewards for Students	Rewards for Parents	Rewards for Teachers
Student-led conferences encourage students • to take an active role in their own learning • to make selections that showcase their own work • to be independent, self-directed learners • to be self-assessors and goal setters • to tell a story about themselves as learners • to learn a real-life skill • to take pride in their own achievements • to have self-confidence and self-esteem	Student-led conferences encourage parents • to become active participants in the conference • to become more aware of the curriculum and its outcomes • to be proud of the student's achievement, regardless of level • to recognize and help students attain goals • to be aware that they are a part of a community of learners • to attend conferences without intimidation • to view learning as a continuum • to view actual products that make up the report card marks	Student-led conferences encourage teachers • to teach in an interactive way • to let students in on the secrets of assessment • to share responsibility of conference with students • to examine ways to improve instruction • to assess the programs, curricula and grade level rubrics • to raise and maintain high expectations • to think about the whole assessment process as an integral part of instruction • to relinquish some of the control in the evaluation process • to have supportive material ready for the report card marks

June 18. This is the end of the fourth year of the portfolio program in our school, and, as a staff, we can really see our own progress. When we look at the cumulative portfolios, we can see their value because we have tracked the progress of students for four years. There have been times when we couldn't see the forest for the trees, so to speak, but we persevered in spite of all the staff changes, curriculum changes and in-service demands on our time. To date, Kay and I have facilitated ten workshops in our own school and thirty-four workshops in other schools. The sharing of ideas and the questions from hundreds of teachers has been our impetus for further learning.

Shirley-Dale

6

Using the Life-Long Learner Model: One School's Story

A good school for me is a place in which everyone
is teaching and everyone is learning simultaneously,
under the same roof. Students are teaching and
learning; principals are teaching and learning; teachers
are teaching and learning.

— Roland Barth

September 10. This is our seventh year of vigilance over the portfolio assessment project. We have been advancing the theory, slowly but steadily, in our school and in the province. Sometimes it seems to me that making a change in a school system is like trying to move a huge amorphous animal standing on the road. Educators come out in droves to heave and tug, to push and shove. Eventually, they get it to budge, and, with all of their might and main, they hold it there until the change begins. But, alas, as soon as they take their hands away, it settles back to where it was, in exactly the same position, resolute, immovable. Yet we are determined to keep at it. We have researched extensively and have learned that systems have changed, but only when the people in charge of them change. That means changing attitudes, values, understandings and beliefs. But how do you do it? We have developed a model that we call the Life-Long Learner Model based on all we have learned. We have been using it in its entirety in our workshops, and, thus far, we have had considerable success.

Shirley-Dale

Implementing and Sustaining New Initiatives

The challenge of implementing and then sustaining new initiatives with a whole staff has been perplexing educators for many years. How do we bring about basic change in schools, and what must we do to make it last? Before embarking on a new initiative as a whole-staff approach, it is important to pay attention to current research regarding the elements that contribute to changing one's fundamental understandings and beliefs.

The following "Life-Long Learner Model" is a framework that identifies these factors. It is circular to symbolize the continuous and cyclical nature of learning.

Life-Long Learner Model

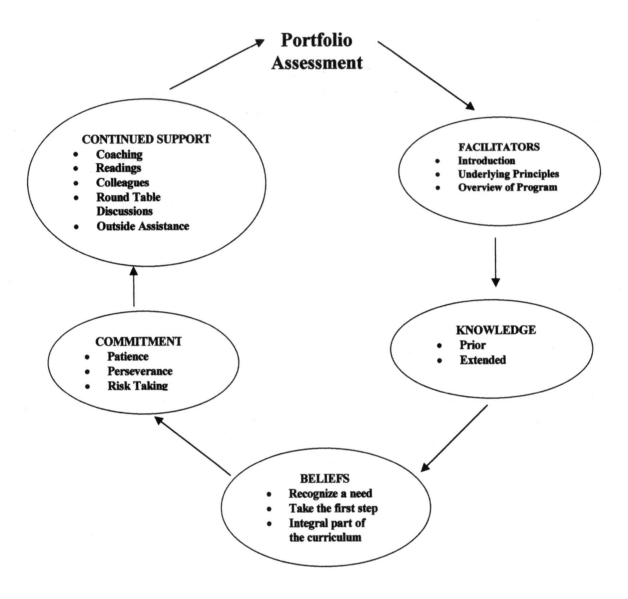

Recognizing the need – The first step in any new initiative is for someone to recognize the need for change in knowledge, understanding, behaviors or skills in a specific area.

Facilitators – The person, or preferably a team of persons, who recognized the need takes the responsibility of becoming a facilitative leader or facilitator. The facilitators must have a clear vision of the end results and be able to articulate how to transfer that vision into practice. Through research, reading and studying current literature, visiting sites where the new initiative is in practice and talking to experts in the field, the facilitators develop a plan of implementation. They gather a well-organized collection of research articles, videos, indexes and computer databases for resources. The next step is to introduce the project, identify the underlying principles and give an overview of the program to the participants.

Knowledge – It is imperative that the facilitators determine the knowledge base of each individual in a group of learners. In this case, teachers are the learners. Like students in any classroom, they are invariably at different stages of development and understanding. Often the success or failure of an initiative is directly related to the attention that is paid to this one factor. It is a wise plan of action to value their prior knowledge and use it to set the stage for collegial interchange and further study. Facilitative leaders provide pertinent research and literature to extend the knowledge of each participant at his or her own level. Time must be allotted for sharing, discussing and clarifying the proposed ideas.

Belief in the initiative – Individuals must believe in the need for a change initiative before they will be willing to get involved. Current practices must be scrutinized and evaluated for effectiveness before teachers can make that decision. The change initiative has to meet their real needs and the possibilities of the situation. Once that is established, the next strategy is to empower the participants to be actively involved in their own learning process. They become co-researchers, critical thinkers and problem solvers as they plan, direct and make decisions in the initial steps of implementation.

Commitment to the project – Patience, perseverance and risk-taking are key elements in the quest to establish and sustain a desired change. The facilitators monitor the progress of and acquire structured and open-ended feedback from the participants in order to keep the interest high. Problems are inherent in any new endeavor, but working through these problems is how progress is made. Participants, at this stage, are vulnerable and susceptible to discouragement so they need to be recognized for their efforts and contributions to the project. They need praise, encouragement and regular reminders of the vision if they are to continue learning and to make a long-term commitment.

Continued support for staff during the initiative – This is the coaching phase. Follow-up support is crucial and is the component that is often missing in staff development, contributing to the downfall of many initiatives. A support system helps to grow roots so a desired change becomes established and sustained. An administrator, in partnership with the facilitators, is responsible for monitoring and assessing progress, refining the course of action and overseeing its continued success. Round table dialogue with colleagues, formal and informal feedback, readings, research and outside assistance are all strategies that will help ensure a higher degree of implementation.

How do you deal with the situation if one or two teachers don't believe in the new initiative?

It is a reality, when working with a large group of people, that not all participants are going to "buy into" the project at the same time. When a teacher does not believe in a concept, there may be a number of reasons.

A teacher might be new to the staff and has not shared in the initial planning and in-service necessary to begin the procedure. It is wise to review and revisit the process and to have current research available at the beginning of each school year. Any teachers new to the initiative can be paired with an experienced teacher on staff as a mentor.

Other times, a teacher might not share the same philosophy of learning and is not ready or willing to change his or her methods. Although this should not curtail the practice for the rest of the school, it may alter the effectiveness of the program.

Quick Tip

"The group must honor the individual; the individual must honor the group."

Michael Fullan

Quick Tip

We routinely ask our children, "What did you learn at school today?" I think it is every bit as important to ask ourselves, "What did I learn at school today?"

Roland Barth

For example, with a portfolio program, when one teacher opts out of the process, it results in a gap in the records of the students' growth. The administration, at this point, might intervene with the help of the facilitators. The teacher may require additional time and support to further his or her studies and to gain confidence. By monitoring that teacher's progress and encouraging each attempt the teacher makes, the whole-staff initiative should move closer to successful implementation.

How can a school get all the teachers on a staff motivated and interested in portfolio assessment?

A good facilitator will be aware of the differences in attitude and levels of learning of all participants and will plan the meetings to allow for as much input as possible from each member. There will always be teachers who need more time for reflection, for reading pedagogy and for making a critical analysis of the idea.

September 3. We had an excellent day today. When we arrived at the main entrance of the school where we were giving our workshop, there was a big welcome sign with our names on it. We could actually feel the energy of the teachers in the room as we began. One of the most encouraging things for us, and we think even more important to the staff, was that the principal and vice principal were in attendance for the entire workshop. We feel that their attendance sent a message to the staff that the implementation of portfolio assessment is a priority and that they, too, are making a personal commitment.

Kay

Is it necessary to have administrative support?

The key to the success of any endeavor is good leadership. It is important that administrators are strong advocates of teacher learning. Principals hold the key to implementing effective change in a school. By assuming a proactive role, they forge the path to change. It is important that they have a well-defined vision of what is needed to improve student learning.

The reality is that the business of managing a school is time-consuming and demanding, and principals may not have the time they would like to devote to staff professional development. A teacher, or small group of teachers, usually has more time to concentrate on issues for professional development. They may wish to present their ideas and plans to the principal and ask permission to act as leaders or facilitators. The principal, if he or she agrees, becomes a member of the team and respects and supports the leaders. On the other hand, the principal or other administrator may, with consultation, appoint a teacher or group of teachers to facilitate the initiative.

Regardless of who spearheads an initiative, the principal remains the one who has the power to implement the change. The responsibility of visiting classrooms and observing what is really happening is that of the principal. No matter how advanced, innovative or creative the classroom teachers are, they do not have the power to assess and effect change in other classrooms without the principal's full support.

How important is it to have outside expertise when beginning the initiative?

Outside expertise lends credibility to a project. It is not always necessary to reinvent the wheel. Consultants have obviously concentrated on just that particular subject for a long time, and it is second nature for them to deal with any questions or problems related to the subject that arise. They have done the basic groundwork and can serve to cement the concept already being discovered. They have the underlying pedagogy and a sharpened vision of the end product. Consultants can motivate the staff to progress faster by opening their eyes to a larger picture.

Is there proof that the "Life-Long Learner Model" works in a real situation, such as the implementation of a portfolio program?

Yes, there is proof. Research abounds with cases of schools achieving moderate to excellent success in staff development using the elements outlined in the framework of the Life-Long Learner Model. Many variables will influence each new initiative, but, basically, paying attention to the essential points in the Life-Long Learner Model makes the difference in the success or failure in implementing a change in a school.

From the Files

The Road to Collaboration — Our Own School's Story

Recognition of the need – In a quiet neighborhood on the outskirts of the city stands our school. It is not formidable or grand, but a simple brick building that houses about one hundred elementary students. As teachers, we had been together for a number of years with few staff changes, and, consequently, had come to know each other well. Over the course of time, we had been chosen, as a whole school, to pilot a number of projects and to report back to a university, the department of education or to another educational faction that needed our input. Willingly, we worked together, sharing ideas and chatting our way through professional development sessions and visits to each other's classrooms. We also were recognized for initiating and developing our own projects to enhance and extend curricula.

Then one day the provincial department of education requested that each school staff-member respond to a series of questions regarding our views on educational philosophy in the early years. After two or three sessions of round-table dialogue, it was apparent that we differed greatly on some major points. This was actually the first time that we began to think about and question our fundamental beliefs about how children learn. For a staff that seemed so congenial in previous endeavors, this was quite disturbing. Where was the dissent coming from? This was not a surface thing. We were all firm in our views, which, we realized, related directly to our values. Uneasiness crept into our workplace, and we seemed divided into separate camps of thinking.

There was only one thing to do in this case: Meet the problem head on. The aftermath of those first debates led us to delve deeper into the exact same subject that caused the dissension: our values and beliefs about how children learn. As two of the teachers on the staff, we decided to take the initiative to help remedy the situation. The easiest way seemed to be to pick a subject and examine our expectations closely. We asked teachers to gather three samples of students' writing from each class, one deemed excellent, one acceptable and one weak. We made overheads of the samples and facilitated a whole-staff discussion about the levels of writing. The differences in what we each called "good writing" were monumental.

Facilitators – What were we going to do to change the situation? We decided to examine the ways we were evaluating and assessing student learning. After discussion with our principal, we received permission to facilitate five workshops on assessment. This was not because we were experts on assessment. As a matter of fact, we had no more knowledge at the time than the rest of the teachers, but we did see the need to change and collaborate. We had just attended a staff development program entitled "Frameworks" and were excited about a co-researching model that was outlined in articles by Brian Cambourne and Jan Turnbill. It is a form of collaborative inquiry that involves all participants and in which everyone has equal status. All parties are acknowledged as having different kinds of expertise, all of which are valued. We decided to take the responsibility for initiating the co-research enterprise in our school. It was the start of a long and interesting journey.

Knowledge – We decided to tailor our five workshops to the needs and beliefs of our school. We were careful to plan the workshops to be exactly one hour in duration. In the first session, we had to define what assessment practices were already in place in our classrooms and what type of information we were obtaining from these types of assessment. It became immediately clear that students played no part in the process.

We gathered a number of research articles on portfolio assessment and divided the teachers into groups of two. Each group was given a different article. The strategic plan was to choose which teachers worked together. We decided to place teachers together who did not necessarily share the same educational philosophy. They had one week to read the article and to reflect on and answer these open-ended questions: "What, in your mind, is the central message in the article? What challenged or confused you? Did anything make you question your previous beliefs?"

Each pair of teachers met to discuss the article and to prepare a small presentation. In the next session, each pair presented their findings. After each report, there was a group discussion. Some heated arguments arose, but we saw the necessity of allowing this debate and discussion to evolve and play itself out. To feel comfortable enough to argue one's beliefs in a forum of professionals is a step in itself toward collaboration. We considered the showing of emotion to be a healthy part of the whole process. These discussions and the written answers to the questions we had asked regarding the articles about portfolio assessment provided us with invaluable insights into the actual attitudes and stages of learning of each teacher. From there, we would have to work out a plan of collaboration for the whole staff. We asked them, quite simply, "What would you like to know? What do we need to answer before we can get started with portfolio assessment in our classrooms?" We then proceeded, as facilitators, to categorize their questions and plan the rest of the workshops accordingly.

Belief in the initiative – One of the concerns was whether portfolio assessment was just another add-on, a flash-in-the-pan kind of thing. Were we embarking on just another *ad-hoc* initiative that had no curriculum connections or long-reaching consequences?

We invited a speaker from the Evaluation Branch of the department of education to come to our third session and speak from a broad perspective about the implications of portfolios in the bigger picture. He told us that in the outside world, employers are no longer asking for well-drilled individuals, they are asking for creative, critical thinkers. Résumés are not enough; portfolios, as evidence of what a person can do, are becoming necessary in many workplaces. He confirmed our beliefs and praised us on the endeavor as a staff to begin teaching this skill in our classrooms. This was a good morale-booster and served as motivation and encouragement for us to continue our research.

How do we reach a common ground when assessing students' work? This was another of the prevalent questions posed by our staff. We decided to assess the same student writing samples that we used in the initial workshop and to try to align our expectations. We used the writing criteria used for provincial assessment and evaluated again, piece by piece. This time we evaluated the level of proficiency, using a common standard. That was what we were lacking before. While examining our expectations, we discovered that low expectations of student performance were leading to low standards. We came to the realization that the students would benefit from evaluating their own writing, using a similar procedure. We decided to follow our students' progress from year to year, using writing samples to show evidence of growth and to teach them to play a part in the process. The decisions that were made during this session led to the first breakthrough in our pursuit for collaboration. This was the step that led to implementing portfolio assessment.

In the final session, we examined what was reasonably possible to accomplish in the first year of implementing portfolio assessment. We reviewed all of the questions and set out a long-term plan. There were many things to iron out. These workshops were only the beginning of the whole initiative. We knew this change in assessment must evolve over a period of time.

Commitment to the project and staff support – Year after year, we plotted the course over roads that were not always familiar. Often backtracking, maneuvering around roadblocks, asking for and mapping out new directions, we were determined to arrive at our destination. Seven years later, the grade 6 students in our school had complete cumulative portfolios as representations of their elementary school years' work. Their selections, with reflections and goals, were rich accumulations of evidence that attested to a seven-year journey of progress. We traveled the road side by side, teachers, students and parents, each gaining skills and insights that we will use long after the trip is over. Or is the journey just beginning?

November 18. This is the first snow of the season. Sitting at the computer, watching the cars sliding in the slush on the streets below, we are thinking back to the beginnings of the long journey that led us to write this book. How important it was that first November night to find that we shared the same vision! This allowed us to explore, debate, disagree, agree, collaborate and share with others. We have covered a lot of ground, both physically and educationally. The road has not always been smooth, but we have managed to forge ahead or to start again with perseverance, determination and a good deal of laughter. Now, we are ready to go to press. To all of the students we have taught, to the parents who have supported us and to all of the educators we have encountered, we say, "Thank-you. You have been our inspiration."

Kay and Shirley-Dale

Resources

Atlantic Canada Mathematics Curriculum. (1999) New Brunswick Department of Education, Curriculum Development Branch, Fredericton, N.B., Canada.

Aker, Don. (1995) *Hitting the Mark: Assessment Tools For Teachers*, Markham, Ontario: Pembroke Publishers Limited.

Bush, R. N. (1984) "Effective Staff Development In Making Our Schools More Effective." Proceeding of three state conferences, San Francisco. Far West Laboratory.

Barth, Roland S. and Deborah Meier. (2001) *Learning by Heart*, San Francisco: Jossey-Bass.

Barth, Roland S. (1990) *Improving Schools from Within*, San Francisco: Jossey-Bass.

Booth, David. (1994) *Classroom Voices: Language-Based Learning in the Elementary School*, Toronto: Harcourt Brace.

Clemmons, J. (1993) *Portfolios in the Classroom: (Grades 1-6),* New York: Scholastic.

Countryman, Joan. (1992) *Writing to Learn Mathematics*, Portsmouth, New Hampshire: Heineman.

Depree, Helen and Sandra Iversen. (1994) *Early Literacy in the Classroom*, Richmond Hill, Ontario: Scholastic Canada.

Ellam-Wason, Linda. (1994) *Literacy Moments to Report Cards*, Markham, Ontario: Pembroke Publishers Limited.

First Steps, Writing Resource Book, (1996) Addison Wesley Longman, Australia Pty Limited, Melbourne, Australia.

Fullan, Michael. (1991) *Change Forces,* New York: Teachers College Press.

Goodman, Y. M. (1993) "Kid-watching: An Alternative to Testing" *National Elementary School Principals,* 57, 4: 41-45.

Grant, J., Heffler, B., and K. Mereweather. (1995) *Student-Led Conferences,* Markham, Ontario: Pembroke Publishing Limited.

Lucas, C. (1990) "Introduction: Writing portfolios—changes and challenges." In K. Yancey (Ed.), *Portfolios in the Writing Classroom.* Urbana, IL. National Council of Teachers of English.

Mathematic Assessment. (1991) edited by Jean Kerr Stenmark, National Council of Teachers of Mathematics, Reston, Virginia.

McMahan, Gale A. and Ann Gifford. (2001) "Portfolios: Achieving Your Personal Best," *The Delta Kappa Gamma Bulletin,* Volume 68

Morgan, Norah and Juliana Saxton. (1994) *Asking Better Questions,* Markham, Ontario: Pembroke Publishers Limited.

Stiggins, R. (1997) *Student-Centered Classroom Assessment* (2nd ed.), Upper Saddle River, NY: Prentice Hall.

Student WEA Resources: "Technology and Portfolio Assessment" http://www.student-wea.org/misc/techport.htm

Teacher Manual for Assessment, Evaluation and Reporting — Elementary. (2000) Ottawa-Carleton District School Board, Ontario, Canada.

Turbill, Jan and Butler, Andrea and Brian Cambourne. (1993) "Teacher As Co-Researcher: How An Approach To Research Became The Methodology For Staff Development," in *Frameworks.* Stanley, N.Y., U.S.A.: Wayne-Finger Lakes Board Cooperative Educational Services.

Van De Walle, John A. (1994) *Elementary School Mathematics: Teaching Developmentally,* White Plains, N.Y.: Longman.

Index